Learning the Battle of Gettysburg

A Guide to the Official Records

by Benjamin Y. Dixon, Ph.D.

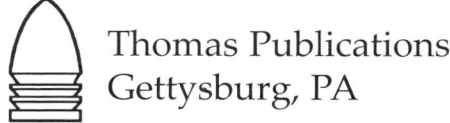

Thomas Publications
Gettysburg, PA

THOMAS PUBLICATIONS publishes books about the American Colonial era, the Revolutionary War, the Civil War, and other important topics. For a complete list of titles, please visit our website:

http://www.thomaspublications.com

Or write to:

THOMAS PUBLICATIONS
P.O. Box 3031
Gettysburg, PA 17325

Copyright © 2007 Benjamin Y. Dixon

Printed and bound in the United States of America

Published by   THOMAS PUBLICATIONS
P.O. Box 3031
Gettysburg, Pa. 17325

All rights reserved. No part of this book may be used or reproduced without written permission of the author and the publisher, except in the case of brief quotations embodied in critical essays and reviews.

ISBN-978-1-57747-121-9

CONTENTS

Using This Guide 4

Chapter 1   Overview & Background of the Battle 7

Chapter 2   The First Day 15

Chapter 3   The Second Day 30

Chapter 4   The Third Day 68

Chapter 5.   Aftermath of the Battle 89

Chapter 6.   Miscellaneous Incidents & Events 100

Chapter 7   Interesting Quotes From the Soldiers 108

Chapter 8   The Organization of the Armies 121

Using This Guide

John B. Bachelder, the most famous of early Gettysburg battlefield guides, relied most heavily on the Official Records to write the Federal Government's history of the battle.

This guide to the Battle of Gettysburg is designed for both the serious enthusiast and the novice. The serious enthusiast is sure to find in this work a treasure-trove of useful information regarding primary sources, notes, quotes, and details about the battle to help enrich their knowledge immensely. The novice is sure to find this work to be most helpful in learning the battle from the very participants who fought in it.

The Battle of Gettysburg is the most written about battle in American literature. Several dozen books on the battle are published every year alone. And yet, to date, the single best primary source on the battle remains the collection of original battle reports submitted by veteran officers and printed in *The War of the Rebellion: Official Records of the Union and Confederate Armies*, Volume 27, parts 1 and 2 (first published in 1889). In fact, these records are the most heavily used source by the Licensed Battlefield Guides at Gettysburg National Military Park.

The *Official Records* contain 356 Union officer reports and 145 Confederate officer reports for the Battle of Gettysburg. No better source gives the true nature of combat than these explicit reports. Readers will find therein shocking descriptions about the carnage and destruction of the battle, about the uncertainty and confusion of the fight, and about the tremendous bravery of many still unknown heroes. Among the most fascinating descriptions are candid comments about incidents of cowardice, death by friendly-fire, the dangers of retrieving the wounded, disputes between officers and units over honors won on the field, and much, much more.

The *Official Records* remain in print and are widely available, but until now, no useful guide existed for finding the right battle reports quickly and easily. When the soldiers, for example, wrote their reports of fighting at "Little Round Top," "Devil's Den," or other now famous places, many did not know or use these place names in their reports. And because they submitted more than 2000 pages of reports, trying to find the very reports that pertain to a particular battle event or place has long proven to be daunting and time-consuming. Worse, the reports were arranged in the *Official Records* according to the Armies' organization of command rather than the chronology of the battle, and printed without a good index. This guide solves all of these problems.

This guide is an annotated index to the *Official Records* for Gettysburg and organized geographically and chronologically to follow the order of battle as it unfolded on the battlefield. In the following pages, Volume 27, parts 1 and 2, of the *Official Records* are referred to as OR 1 or OR 2. Numbers following these designations are page numbers within each respective volume. Readers are able to learn which reports and parts of reports pertain to nearly every significant battle event from the opening of the fight to its aftermath (see Chapters 1 through 5). Please note that reports designated with (**) are particularly vivid in description or offer an excellent explanation of events. In addition, other fascinating incidents and commentary by the soldiers have been indexed herein (see Chapter 6). Also, this guide provides a substantial selection of the best and most interesting quotes written by the soldiers that further illustrate the battle (see Chapter 7). And finally, a more complete "Order of Battle" has been appended (see Chapter 8) showing all participating units from both armies, the nicknames of key units, and all reports referenced to the units that submitted them.

Perhaps most fascinating to readers as they peruse the following pages will be the variance in coverage of the battle by the *Official Records*. There are instances where some events or units significant to the battle are ignored or barely mentioned by the reports. In other cases, the amount of report coverage concerning a particular event (such as the cannonade preceding Pickett's Charge) is astonishing! In Chapter 8, I purposely added OR page references to reveal which units had considerable report coverage, and which did not. Moreover, some reports have even been revised, others contain exaggerations, and occasional errors exist due to the confusion of battle or latent memory. But any such variance in no way detracts from the value of the *Official Records*. The reports that are included, and what is in them, offer the reader incredible drama and insight into the greatest battle of America's Civil War.

The official Gettysburg battle reports are the words and memories of battery, regiment, brigade, division, and corps commanders of both sides, as well as the army commanders themselves — Union Army of the Potomac General George G. Meade and Confederate Army of Northern Virginia General Robert E. Lee. Through their descriptions of the battle we can see the battlefield as they saw it, learn the combat as they felt it, and be intrigued by what they most remembered from their traumatic experiences at Gettysburg. These reports are their legacy.

Benjamin Y. Dixon
21 May 2006

1

Overview & Background of the Battle

Gettysburg is "the hardest fought battle of the war in which I have been engaged..."

Gettysburg was a complex battle. Any understanding of it must begin with an overview before delving deeper into the subject. This chapter provides the reports and parts of those reports that give readers the best introduction to the battle, its causes, and the armies. Included herein are the size and organization of the armies, the times of their arrival, and the weaponry and tactics they employed.

Best Overall Reports on the Battle

The following are the most comprehensive reports on the Gettysburg campaign. To reference them throughout the remaining chapters would prove too repetitive. They are concentrated here and should always be consulted in addition to the reports referenced for specific events listed in all chapters.

OR 1: 61-74, 114-121 (Gen. Meade's Report)
OR 1: 228-243 (Gen. Hunt's Report)
OR 1: 367-377 (Gen. Hancock's Report)
OR 1: 697-711 (Gen. Howard's Report)
OR 1: 914-916 (Gen. Pleasonton's Report) — see battlefield map, p. 915.
OR 2: 298-303; 307-311; 313-325 (Gen. Lee's Report)
OR 2: 348-353 (Gen. Pendleton's Report)
OR 2: 357-361 (Gen. Longstreet's Report)
OR 2: 444-448 (Gen. Ewell's Report)
OR 2: 464-473 (Gen. Early's Report)
OR 2: 552-559 (Gen. Rodes' Report)

July 1

A Confederate Victory
OR 1: 243-257 (Gen. Doubleday's Report)
OR 1: 701-704 (Gen. Howard's Report)
OR 1: 727-730 (Gen. Schurz's Report)
OR 2: 468-470 (Gen. Early's Report)

July 2

Strategy & Outcome: Attacking the Flanks, Stalemate
OR 1: 828-833 (Gen. Geary's Report)
OR 2: 446-447 (Gen. Ewell's Report)

July 3

Strategy & Outcome: Attacking the Center, Victory & Defeat
OR 2: 359-360 (Gen. Longstreet's Report)

Causes of the Battle

Strategic Importance of Gettysburg as Hub of Roads
OR 1: 246-247 (Gen. Doubleday's Report)
OR 1: 697-700 (Gen. Howard's Report) — see map of 12 roads, p. 699.

Size of Armies

OR 1: 154 (Union)
OR 2: 292 (Confederate) — incomplete.

Command Structure Among Infantry Officers

For efficient reading, this guide addresses all Generals and Colonels as such, without distinguishing their specific level within these ranks, however, full rank title for officers is found in Chapter 8.

General, Lieutenant General, Major General, Brigadier General, Colonel, Lieutenant Colonel, Major, Captain, First Lieutenant, Second Lieutenant.

Organization of the Armies

UNION ARMY OF THE POTOMAC — Seven infantry corps, one cavalry corps, & one artillery reserve.

Corps — consisting most often of three, sometimes two, divisions and one artillery brigade.

Division — consisting most often of three, sometimes two, brigades. One division had four brigades.

Brigade — consisting most often of four, sometimes five, regiments. Ranged from three to seven regiments.

Regiment — consisting most often of ten companies organized into two battalions. The First Battalion of five companies was led by the Lt. Colonel of the regiment, and the Second Battalion was led be the Major. The two battalions were referred to as "Left Wing" and "Right Wing." Also, a regiment with less than ten companies total was sometimes referred to as a "battalion."

Company — unit of 100 soldiers at war's outset prior to sustaining casualties.

CONFEDERATE ARMY OF NORTHERN VIRGINIA — Three infantry corps & one cavalry corps.

Corps — consisting of three divisions and one artillery reserve (of two battalions).

Division — consisting most often of four, sometimes five, brigades and one artillery battalion. Ranged from three to six brigades.

Brigade — consisting most often of five, sometimes four or six, regiments. A few had only three regiments.

Regiment — same as above.

Company — same as above.

Army Size & Organization

Union — Army of the Potomac	
Total Size	Approximately 93,000
Corps	*Total*: 7 Infantry, plus 1 Cavalry, and 1 Artillery Reserve. Average Size: 10,000 – 13,000 men. Each Corps had 2-3 Divisions, 1 Artillery Brigade, and shared Artillery Reserve.
Division	*Total*: 19 Infantry & 3 Cavalry Average Size: 3,000 – 4,000 men Usually 2-3 brigades
Brigade	*Total*: 51 Infantry & 8 Cavalry Average Size: 1400 men Usually 4-5 regiments
Regiment	*Total*: 242 Infantry & 31 Cavalry Average Size: 250 – 350 men Usually 10 companies or less
Company	*Average size*: 25 – 35 men
Artillery	1 Artillery Reserve for the Army, consisting of 5 Artillery Brigades, operated to be shared by all 7 Infantry Corps. Artillery Reserve was equivalent to Division. 1 additional Brigade per Corps, usually of 4-5 batteries. Battery averaged 6 guns. Brigade averaged 24-30 guns. Chief of Artillery claimed 320 guns served, excluding Cavalry which had 46 guns in the battle. *Total*: 65 Batteries, 366 guns.
Cavalry	3 Divisions (totaling 8 brigades), and 1 Horse Artillery Unit (comprised of 2 Artillery Brigades).

CONFEDERATE — ARMY OF NORTHERN VIRGINIA	
Total Size	Approximately 75,000
Corps	*Total*: 3 Infantry, plus 1 Cavalry Division, and 3 Artillery Reserve Units. Average Size: 20,000 – 22,000 men. Each Corps had 3 Divisions (including 3 Artillery Battalions) and 1 Artillery Reserve unit.
Division	*Total*: 9 Infantry & 1 Cavalry Average Size: 6,000 – 8,000 men Usually 4-5 brigades & 1 Artillery Battalion
Brigade	*Total*: 37 Infantry & 7 Cavalry Average Size: 1600 men Usually 4-6 regiments
Regiment	*Total*: 171 Infantry & 29 Cavalry Average Size: 300 – 400 men Usually 10 companies or less
Company	*Average size*: 30 – 40 men
Artillery	Artillery Reserve, totalling 6 Artillery Battalions, was split into 3 parts — giving 1 Artillery Reserve unit per Corps, consisting of 2 Battalions each. 3 additional Battalions per Corps, split into 1 Battalion per Division, usually of 4-5 batteries. Battery averaged 4 guns. Battalion averaged 16 guns. Chief of Artillery claimed 241 guns served, excluding Cavalry which had 33 guns in the battle. *Total*: 70 Batteries, 274 guns.
Cavalry	1 Division (totaling 6 brigades), plus 1 separate brigade, and 1 Horse Artillery Unit (1 Artillery Battalion).

Time of Arrival of the Armies

UNION ARMY OF THE POTOMAC
  Buford's Cavalry Division — About 11:00 a.m. on June 30.
  1st Corps — Began arriving after 10:00 a.m. of July 1.
  11th Corps — Began arriving about noon of July 1.
  2nd Corps — Began arriving at 4:00 p.m. and into evening, July 1.
  12th Corps — Began arriving at 5:00 p.m. and into evening, July 1.
  3rd Corps — Began arriving evening of July 1 and into early morning of July 2.
  General Meade — Arrived around 1:00 a.m. on July 2.
  5th Corps — Began arriving around 8:00 a.m. on July 2.
  Pleasonton's Cavalry — Gregg's and Kilpatrick's Divisions arrived noon of July 2.
  6th Corps — Arrived afternoon, July 2 after marching over 30 miles.

CONFEDERATE ARMY OF NORTHERN VIRGINIA
  Early's Division — Arrived June 26th and returned to Gettysburg about 2:30 p.m. on July 1.
  Pettigrew's Brigade — Arrived briefly on June 30th and returned to Cashtown where Heth's and Pender's Divisions of Hill's Corps awaited until the next morning.
  Hill's Corps — Heth's and Pender's Divisions arrived in the morning of July 1, and Anderson's Division arrived late that afternoon around 5:00 p.m.
  Ewell's Corps — Rodes' Division arrived around Noon on July 1, Early's Division follows thereafter, & Johnson's Division arrived late that night.
  General Lee — Arrived afternoon of July 1.
  Longstreet's Corps — Arrived night of July 1 and moved into position July 2.
  Stuart's Cavalry — Arrived late afternoon of July 2.

> Stuart's cavalry passed between the Union Army and Washington, D.C. in an attempt to divert Federal attention away from Lee's Army moving north. On June 27, Stuart proceeded north from Fairfax Court House, Virginia, across the Potomac River to Rockville, Maryland (June 28), where he captured more than 125 Federal wagons. His cavalry proceeded to Westminster (June 29), and then to Hanover, Pennsylvania, where he clashed with Kilpatrick's Union cavalry on June 30. From there, the

Confederate cavalry went to Carlisle, arriving on the afternoon of July 1, and headed to Gettysburg the next day, arriving there in the late afternoon.

OR 2: 692-697, 708-709, 711 (Gen. Stuart's Report) — see map on p. 711.

Weaponry & Tactics

Small Arms & Ammunition
OR 1: 388 (Capt. Touhy's Report) — Smoothbore Springfield musket .69 cal.
OR 1: 460 (Col. Carpenter's Report) — Capturing Springfield rifles from Rebels.
OR 1: 655-656 (Gen. Crawford's Report**) — See "list of arms captured" p. 656.
OR 1: 840 (Col. Patrick's Report) — Smokeless & flashless air rifles of Rebels.
OR 2: 697 (Gen. Stuart's Report) — Jenkins' Cavalry used "Enfield muskets."

Artillery & Ammunition
OR 1: 241 (Gen. Hunt's Report**) — Union army used 6 types of cannon, especially 12-pdr. Napoleons, 3-inch Rifles, and Parrott guns.
OR 1: 588 (Capt. Smith's Report) — Use of shot, case, shell, and canister.
OR 1: 590-591 (Lieut. James' Report) — Use of shot, spherical case, and canister. Common cannon used were 3-inch ordnance rifles and 12-pdr. Napoleons. Ammunition was stored in limbers and caissons.
OR 1: 754-755 (Capt. Dilger's Report**)
OR 1: 757 (Lieut. Bancroft's Report) — See table on ammunition expended.
OR 1: 872-876 (Gen. Tyler's Report)
OR 1: 878-879 (Lieut. Gillett's Report**)
OR 1: 887-888 (Capt. Hart's Report**)
OR 1: 892-893 (Capt. Edgell's Report**)
OR 2: 355-356 (Addenda to Gen. Pendleton's Report**) — Confederates used seven types of cannon, notably 12-pdr. Napoleons, 3-inch Rifles, Parrott guns, and Howitzers.
OR 2: 357 (Col. Baldwin's Report**) — Confederates lost zero cannon and captured seven Union guns during the battle.
OR 2: 381 (Capt. Manly's Report) — There are eight gunners to every gun, each with a number. Read about Private Thain who is "No. 6" and responsible for igniting fuses.
OR 2: 458-459 (Lieut. Gregory's Report**) — Comments on damage to guns, and the dangers and problems with Confederate ammunition.
OR 2: 587-588 (Gen. Ramseur's Report) — Union guns could fire "direct, cross, and enfilade" upon his lines. These were the three types of direction of cannon fire: "Direct" meaning fire to come from the front, "cross" (or "oblique") meaning being struck from the diagonals which creates a crossfire, and "enfilade" meaning the fire is coming from the flanks.

OR 2: 612 (Col. Walker's Report**) — See table on ammunition expended.

OR 2: 635-636 (Maj. Lane's Report**) — Describes the type of shot often fired by guns, and the dangers and losses to horses and men who operate artillery in battle.

Advance En Masse, En Echelon, Enfilade, March and Deploy by Battalion, Refusing the Line, Retire by Prolonged Fire, and Other Examples of Tactics Used

OR 1: 483 (Gen. Birney's Report) — "advanced en masse"

OR 1: 498 (Col. Tippin's Report) — "deployed ... by battalions"

OR 1: 623 (Col. Chamberlain's Report) — "refusing" the line. See map on p. 619 of Col. Rice's Report for an excellent illustration of this maneuver.

OR 1: 825 (Gen. Geary's Report) — "enfilading"

OR 1: 837 (Col. Candy's Report) — "enfilading fire"

OR 1: 882 (Col. McGilvery's Report) — "retired by prolonge"

OR 2: 368 (Gen. Kershaw's Report) — "directing battalion"

OR 2: 375 (Col. Cabell's Report) — "en echelon"

OR 2: 386 (Maj. Peyton's Report) — "enfiladed nearly our entire line"

OR 2: 392 (Col. Oates' Report) — "left-wheel my regiment"

OR 2: 509 (Gen. Steuart's Report) — "right half-wheel"

OR 2: 608 (Gen. Hill's Report) — "en echelon"

2

The First Day

"...they were fighting on the soil of their native state...."

Major General John Reynolds died on the morning of July 1, 1863, while bringing up his Union troops to stop the Confederate forces arriving west of Gettysburg. He was a Pennsylvanian, one of the best generals in the Union Army of the Potomac, and the highest ranking officer on either side to die in the battle. This chapter provides reports that discuss the opening of the battle and its progress through the first day. Included are the engagements at McPherson Ridge, Oak Ridge, Barlow's Knoll, the Seminary, the Confederate capture of the town, and the fortification of Cemetery Hill.

Gettysburg: June 26-30

In June 1863, General Robert E. Lee advanced his Army of Northern Virginia north via the Shenandoah and Cumberland Valleys into Pennsylvania. Lieutenant General Richard "Dick" Ewell's Corps led with advanced units moving north toward Harrisburg and east to Gettysburg. On June 26, a lead force of Major General Jubal Early's Division of Ewell's Corps entered Gettysburg via the Cashtown Pike after easily routing about 800 of the local 26th Pennsylvania infantry militia near Marsh Creek. No one was killed, but after Early's division occupied the town, some Confederate pickets shot dead a 21st Pennsylvania militia cavalryman named George Sandoe, making him the first Gettysburg fatality. Early subsequently demanded money and supplies from the town (of which little could be found) and burned a few train cars and a bridge before continuing to York.

On June 28, Major General George G. Meade was appointed to replace Major General Joseph Hooker as the new commander of the Union Army of the Potomac, and his army was already moving north through Maryland to intercept Lee. Two days later, advanced Union cavalry units found Confederate forces at Hanover and Gettysburg. At Hanover, on June 30, Brigadier General Judson Kilpatrick's Union cavalry clashed with Confederate cavalry under Major General J.E.B. Stuart who had been leading his men on a daring raid around the Union army and was out of contact with Lee. That same day, Brigadier General John Buford's Union cavalry reached Gettysburg in time to find Confederate troops under Brigadier General J. Johnston Pettigrew approaching just west of town on the Cashtown Pike. Pettigrew had been ordered to Gettysburg by his division commander, Major General Henry Heth. No engagement ensued, and Pettigrew's men returned to Cashtown where Lee had ordered his army to concentrate. Unaware that major Union forces were nearby, Heth's Third Corps commander, Lieutenant General Ambrose P. Hill, determined to "advance the next morning and discover what was in my front" at Gettysburg. There on the ridges west of Gettysburg, Buford's men camped the night of June 30 and prepared to hold their position and the town until Union infantry could arrive the next day.

Early's Raid
  OR 2: 213, 217-219 (Gen. Couch's Report) — See orders by the President and Governor calling for Pennsylvania Militia to help repel the invasion.
  OR 2: 464-465 (Gen. Early's Division Report**) — Early's Division marches with White's & French's cavalry units.

The Clash of Cavalry at Hanover: Kilpatrick finds Stuart
  OR 1: 986-987 (Gen. Kilpatrick's Dispatches)
  OR 1: 992 (Gen. Kilpatrick's Division Report)
  OR 1: 997-1000 (Gen. Custer's Brigade Report)
  OR 1: 1008-1009 (Maj. Hammond's Report** — 5th NY)
  OR 1: 1011 (Maj. Darlington's Report — 18th PA)
  OR 1: 1018 (Maj. Capehart's Report — 1st WV)
  OR 2: 695-696 (Gen. Stuart's Division Report)

Converging Armies: The Arrival of Heth and Buford
  OR 1: 914 (Gen. Pleasonton's Cavalry Corps Report)
  OR 1: 923-924 (Gen. Buford's Dispatches**)
  OR 1: 926-927 (Gen. Buford's Division Report)
  OR 1: 1030 (Lieut. Calef's Battery Report)
  OR 2: 607 (Gen. Hill's III Corps Report**)
  OR 2: 637 (Gen. Heth's Division Report**)

Herr's Ridge and McPherson's Ridge

On July 1, Heth's Confederates left Cashtown around 4:00 a.m. and headed for Gettysburg. When they approached Marsh Creek at about 7:30 a.m., still five miles from town, one of Buford's advanced pickets fired the first shot at them. "For more than two hours," Buford's First Brigade resisted the Confederate advance, but they were far outnumbered. When Heth's men approached Herr's Ridge, one mile west of Gettysburg, they encountered fire from more Federal cavalrymen who were dismounted. Buford's main line stood on McPherson's Ridge with Lieutenant John Calef's Battery. This battery fired the first artillery shot at the approaching Confederates. On the ridge was the McPherson Farm with its white-washed barn that provided cover for both sides and later served as a hospital. After Heth deployed his troops along Herr's Ridge on either side of the Cashtown Pike, the fighting quickly escalated. Buford's men hung on desperately until Federal infantry reached the field.

Shortly after 10:00 a.m., Major General John Reynolds arrived with lead units of his Union 1st Corps infantry. Reynolds was widely considered to be one of the best officers in the Union Army, and under fire he quickly directed his men into action. The first of his troops on the scene were those of Cutler's Brigade whose 56th Pennsylvania fired the first infantry volley at the Rebels. When Confederates of Brigadier General James Archer's brigade entered Herbst Woods, a woodlot immediately south of the McPherson farm, Reynolds sent portions of Brigadier General Solomon Meredith's "Iron Brigade" to stop them. The Iron Brigade pushed the Confederates back and captured many, including General Archer. However, near the eastern edge of the woods, Reynolds was shot in the brain and instantly killed. Those woods have since been remembered in his honor as Reynolds Woods. He was the highest ranking officer casualty of the battle.

OPENING OF THE BATTLE
    OR 1: 265-266 (Gen. Wadsworth's Division Report) — Cutler's Brigade is the first Federal infantry on the scene with General Reynolds.
    OR 1: 281-282 (Gen. Cutler's Brigade Report)
    OR 1: 285 (Capt. Cook's Report — 76th NY)
    OR 1: 288 (Col. Hoffman's Report — 56th PA)
    OR 1: 354-355 (Col. Wainwright's Artillery Report) — Read about Hall's battery.
    OR 1: 359-360 (Capt. Hall's Battery Report**)
    OR 1: 914 (Gen. Pleasonton's Cavalry Corps Report)
    OR 1: 927 (Gen. Buford's Report**) — Read about Calef's battery.
    OR 1: 934-935 (Col. Gamble's Brigade Report)
    OR 1: 938-939 (Col. Devin's Brigade Report)
    OR 1: 1030-1032 (Lieut. Calef's Battery Report**) — Fires the first Union gun in the battle.
    OR 2: 607 (Gen. Hill's III Corps Report)
    OR 2: 610-611 (Col. Walker's Artillery Report)
    OR 2: 637 (Gen. Heth's Division Report**) — "I was ignorant what force was at or near Gettysburg…"
    OR 2: 646 (Col. Shepard's Report — Archer's brigade)
    OR 2: 648-649 (Gen. Davis' Brigade Report)
    OR 2: 674 (Maj. McIntosh's Battalion Report)
    OR 2: 677-678 (Capt. Brunson's Report — Pegram's Battalion)

THE IRON BRIGADE DEFEATS AND CAPTURES GENERAL ARCHER
    OR 1: 245 (Gen. Doubleday's Report)
    OR 1: 267 (Col. Morrow's Report — 24th Michigan)
    OR 1: 273-274 (Maj. Mansfield's Report — 2nd Wisconsin)
    OR 1: 279 (Col. Robinson's Report — 7th WI)
    OR 2: 638 (Gen. Heth's Division Report)
    OR 2: 646 (Col. Shepard's Report — Archer's Brigade)

REYNOLDS WOODS AND REYNOLDS' DEATH
    OR 1: 245 (Gen. Doubleday's I Corps Report)

OR 1: 313 (Gen. Rowley's Report — Doubleday's Div.) — Attributed "much of the ultimate success of our army" to Reynolds' decision to fight at Gettysburg.
OR 1: 327 (Col. McFarland's Report — 151st PA)
OR 1: 355 (Col. Wainwright's Artillery Report)
OR 2: 637 (Gen. Heth's Report) — Heth erroneously claims a shell killed Reynolds.
OR 2: 677 (Capt. Brunson's Report — Pegram's Battalion)

Railroad Cut

An unfinished railroad bed leading west out of Gettysburg had been cut through McPherson Ridge just north of and parallel to the Chambersburg Pike. On the morning of July 1, Brigadier General Joseph Davis' Confederate brigade of Heth's Division advanced from Herr's Ridge across the farm fields north of the railroad bed to attack Union troops deployed there. The attack was furious, and the Confederates pushed the Federals back into the woods on Oak Ridge. In response to this crisis, the 6th Wisconsin regiment led by Lieutenant Colonel Rufus Dawes moved into a position along the south edge of the Chambersburg Pike. Dawes' troops opened fire on the flank of the Confederates, forcing them to seek shelter in the railroad cut as their commander, General Davis, ordered a withdrawal. Seizing the opportunity, Dawes and his troops, along with the 14th Brooklyn and 95th New York regiments, charged to the railroad cut and captured about 240 Confederates of Davis' Brigade. According to Dawes, "...the entire regiment in my front, after some murderous skirmishing by the more desperate, threw down their arms." The charge occurred around 11:00 a.m. General Davis, a nephew of Confederate President Jefferson Davis, was not captured.

BAYONET CHARGE OF RUFUS DAWES' 6TH WISCONSIN
OR 1: 246 (Gen. Doubleday's I Corps Report)
OR 1: 275-276, 278 (Col. Rufus Dawes' Report — 6th WI)
OR 1: 282 (Gen. Cutler's Brigade Report)
OR 1: 286-287 (Col. Fowler's Report — 14th Brooklyn)
OR 1: 287 (Maj. Pye's Report — 95th NY)
OR 2: 637 (Gen. Heth's Division Report)
OR 2: 649 (Gen. Davis' Brigade Report**) — Times given are two hours fast.

Oak Ridge and McPherson's Ridge

Around Noon, the battle had paused, but another Confederate division, under Major General Robert Rodes of Ewell's Corps, arrived on Oak Hill. Under cover of the woods on Oak Hill, Rodes deployed his troops to strike the northern flank of the Union First Corps positioned along Oak Ridge. Lieutenant Colonel Thomas Carter's battalion immediately began an hour-long artillery barrage to enfilade Union guns near the railroad cut and along Seminary Ridge. Seeing Union soldiers in Sheads Woods, Rodes sent three brigades, commanded by Colonel Edward O'Neal and Brigadier Generals Alfred Iverson and Junius Daniel. As O'Neal advanced from Oak Hill, Iverson advanced from the John Forney Farm with Daniel's troops supporting his right. Iverson's Brigade charged across open fields and were torn apart from fire by unseen Federals of Brigadier General Henry Baxter's Brigade positioned "behind a concealed stone wall" along the crest of Oak Ridge. Baxter's troops had already repulsed O'Neal's men and were able to shift and concentrate their fire against Iverson's attack. Many fell in the same formation as they had advanced. General Iverson noted, "...I found afterward that 500 of my men were left lying dead and wounded on a line as straight as a dress parade[.]" Counterchanges by portions of Baxter's troops captured several hundred more of Iverson's men.

Meanwhile, several regiments of Daniel's brigade approached the railroad cut to assault Colonel Roy Stone's Union brigade on the McPherson farm. Stone had positioned two of his regiments along the Chambersburg Pike to stop them, but he could not keep the Confederates out of the railroad cut. Daniel's troops repeatedly attacked Stone's men, but were repulsed as the fighting raged back-and-forth between the cut and the pike, a distance of "about 100 yards." According to one of Stone's officers, "three successive assaults upon our line were repulsed [.]" For a while, all engagements on the field went like this one. The afternoon fighting lasted more than three hours, and every brigade involved from Rodes' Division eventually made two or three attacks before Union forces began to retreat. As many Confederate commanders noted, the Federals "made a stubborn resistance, [before being] finally driven from the field."

By mid-afternoon, General Lee had arrived on the scene. When he saw that Union troops on McPherson's Ridge were being shifted to fight Rodes' Division, he ordered Heth to renew the attack on McPherson's Ridge. Heth sent Brigadier General J. Johnston Pettigrew's and Colonel John Brockenbrough's Confederate brigades to advance on Willoughby Run and strike the Iron Brigade and other Union forces in Herbst Woods. The Confederates greatly outnumbered and outflanked the Federals, but the Union troops resisted. The fighting in the woods was close, sometimes within 20 paces. The Federals were eventually forced out of the woods and east across open fields to Seminary Ridge, all the while "contesting every foot of ground." The stubbornness of both sides is evident by the casualties of the 26th North Carolina and the 24th Michigan regiments who opposed each other along Willoughby Run and in McPherson's Woods. Both regiments could rightfully claim having lost "more than half [their] men killed and wounded." In fact, for the entire battle, each would suffer the highest total regimental losses in their respective armies.

Rodes' Division Fights the 1st Corps
- OR 2: 552-554, 559 (Gen. Rodes' Division Report**) — Rodes' division was complimented by Lee, see p. 559.
- OR 2: 569 (Gen. Daniel's Brigade Report) — Claims division arrives at 1:00 p.m. and fights to 4:00 p.m.
- OR 2: 577-578 (Capt. Van Brown's Report** — 2nd NC Battalion) — Claims fight begins between 12:00 and 1:00 p.m.
- OR 2: 592 (Col. O'Neal's Brigade Report). Carter's artillery duel lasts one hour.
- OR 2: 596 (Col. Hall's Report** — 5th AL) — Description of terrain. Fatigued from the rapid march, Hall's men were brought into battle on the run, causing some men to faint from exhaustion.
- OR 2: 601 (Col. Pickens' Report — 12th AL) — Carter's hour-long artillery duel.

Iverson's Charge
- OR 2: 444-445 (Gen. Ewell's II Corps Report)
- OR 2: 554 (Gen. Rodes' Division Report) — "His dead lay in a distinctly marked line of battle."
- OR 2: 579-580 (Gen. Iverson's Brigade Report**)
- OR 2: 587 (Gen. Ramseur's Brigade Report) — Three regiments annihilated.

The Countercharges of Portions of Baxter's Brigade
- OR 1: 289-290 (Gen. Robinson's Division Report). — "The enemy…[lost] three flags and about 1,000 prisoners."
- OR 1: 292 (Col. Coulter's Report — 11th PA) — Claims 500 prisoners captured.
- OR 1: 307 (Gen. Baxter's Brigade Report)
- OR 1: 310 (Col. Wheelock's Report — 97th NY) — Captured prisoners in two charges.
- OR 1: 311 (Capt. Patterson's Report — 88th PA) — Captured two flags.

Daniel's Brigade Attacks Stone's Brigade from the Railroad Cut
- OR 1: 249-250 (Gen. Doubleday's First Corps Report)
- OR 1: 329-331 (Col. Stone's Brigade Report) — Read about the 149th PA.
- OR 1: 331-333 (Col. Wister's Report — Stone's Brigade) — Read about the 150th PA. Inf.
- OR 1: 334-335 (Col. Dana's Report** — 143rd PA)
- OR 1: 341-343 (Col. Dwight's Report** — 149th PA)
- OR 1: 345 (Capt. Irvin's Report — 149th PA)
- OR 1: 346 (Col. Huidekoper's Report — 150th PA) — Fights from McPherson Farm.

OR 1: 347 (Capt. Jones' Report — 150th PA)
OR 2: 554 (Gen. Rodes' Division Report)
OR 2: 566 (Gen. Daniel's Brigade Report)
OR 2: 571-572 (Col. Brabble's Report — 32nd NC)
OR 2: 574 (Capt. Hopkins' Report — 45th NC)
OR 2: 577-578 (Capt. Van Brown's Report** — 2nd NC Battalion)

CONFEDERATES CLEAR MCPHERSON'S RIDGE
OR 1: 268-269 (Col. Henry Morrow's Report** — 24th Michigan) — The Confederates "came on ... yelling like demons" (p. 268). The 26th North Carolina and Brockenbrough's troops force the Iron Brigade out of McPherson Woods and back to the Seminary.
OR 1: 274 (Maj. Mansfield's Report — 2nd WI)
OR 1: 279-280 (Col. Robinson's Report — 7th WI)
OR 1: 313 (Gen. Rowley's Division Report) — Biddle's Brigade advanced into the fields west of the Seminary to stop Pettigrew's advance but was forced to retire to the Seminary.
OR 1: 315 (Col. Biddle's Brigade Report)
OR 1: 317, 320-321 (Col. Gates' Report** — 20th NYS Militia / 80th NY)
OR 1: 323 (Maj. Biddle's Report — 121st PA)
OR 1: 327-328 (Col. McFarland's Report** — 151st PA)
OR 1: 330 (Col. Stone's Brigade Report)
OR 1: 333-334 (Col. Wister's Report — Stone's Brigade) — Stone's Brigade left McPherson's Ridge after 3 p.m.
OR 1: 335-336 (Col. Dana's Report — 143rd PA) — Dana commanded Stone's Brigade retreat from the McPherson farm and railroad cut, and halted the brigade at Seminary Ridge.
OR 1: 343 (Col. Dwight's Report — 149th PA) — Praised Col. Dana for "most gallant work on the retreat from McPherson's barn to the Seminary".
OR 1: 346-347 (Col. Huidekoper's Report — 150th PA)
OR 1: 362 (Lieut. Breck's Report — Reynolds' Battery)
OR 2: 638-639 (Gen. Heth's Division Report) — The sacrifice of 26th NC.
OR 2: 643 (Maj. Jones' Report** — 26th NC)

McLean's Farm and Barlow's Knoll

East of Oak Ridge stretched a "plain" of open farm fields from the Mummasburg Road to the Harrisburg Road immediately north of the town of Gettysburg. Here in the early afternoon, Shurz's Division of the Union 11th Corps, temporarily commanded by Brigadier General Alexander Schimmelfennig, arrived intent on reinforcing Union 1st Corps troops on Oak Ridge. But on the McLean Farm immediately east of Oak Ridge, Confederates of Brigadier General George Doles' Brigade stood in their way. Doles' Brigade held the far left of Rodes' Division and had deployed across the farm fields to meet the soldiers from the Union 11th Corps who were coming from town. Beginning around 2:00 p.m., Doles' Brigade engaged Schimmelfennig's troops, who outnumbered them. Artillery from Carter's guns on Oak Hill proved critical in helping Doles' men stay the Federals in the open on the McLean farm fields until more Confederates could arrive on the scene.

Meanwhile, another division of the Union 11th Corps, commanded by Brigadier General Francis Barlow, arrived and was ordered to protect Schimmelfennig's right flank. Barlow anchored his troops on a knoll overlooking Rock Creek and the Harrisburg Road. The 11th Corps line was stretched terribly thin. In addition, General Jubal Early's Confederate division of Ewell's Corps had arrived from the north on the Harrisburg Road. At about 3:30 p.m., Early had Brigadier General John B. Gordon's Brigade attack Barlow. As Gordon's troops attacked, Doles' men joined them and they struck the Federal lines simultaneously. Together, they proved an unstoppable force. Within an hour, the two brigades of Georgians had the entire 11th Corps line in retreat through town and General Barlow lay critically wounded.

THE FIGHT OVER MCLEAN'S FARM
   OR 1: 727-729 (Gen. Schurz's Division Report)
   OR 1: 738 (Col. Brown's Report — 157th NY)
   OR 1: 745 (Maj. Ledig's Report — 75th PA)
   OR 1: 747 (Maj. Osborn's Artillery Report) — Read about Dilger's battery.
   OR 1: 752-753 (Lieut. Wheeler's Battery Report)
   OR 1: 754 (Capt. Dilger's Battery Report)
   OR 2: 581-582 (Gen. Doles' Brigade Report**)
   OR 2: 584 (Maj. Willis' Report — 4th GA)
   OR 2: 585-586 (Maj. Peebles' Report** — 44th GA)
   OR 2: 603 (Col. Carter's Battalion Report)

EARLY ATTACKS AND OBLITERATES BARLOW
   OR 1: 715 (Col. Harris' Report — Ames' Brigade)
   OR 1: 728-729 (Gen. Schurz's Division Report)
   OR 1: 748 (Maj. Osborn's Artillery Report) — Bayard Wilkeson's wounding.
   OR 1: 756 (Lieut. Bancroft's Report — Wilkeson's Battery)
   OR 2: 468-469 (Gen. Early's Division Report**)
   OR 2: 492-493 (Gen. Gordon's Brigade Report) — Mentions Barlow's wounding.
   OR 2: 495 (Col. Jones' Battalion Report) — His four cannon were disabled.
   OR 2: 497 (Capt. Green's Battery Report) — How Parrott gun was disabled.
   OR 2: 607 (Gen. Hill's III Corps Report) — Claims Early's Division arrived at 2:30 p.m.

Oak Ridge and Seminary Ridge

Late in the afternoon, the Union army's position was in peril. The 11th Corps was breaking apart and retreating, the 1st Corps was barely managing to stay on Oak Ridge and Seminary Ridge, and more of Lee's army continued to arrive with greater numbers and speed. Major General Abner Doubleday, in command of the Union 1st Corps, later wrote: "About 4 p.m., the enemy …[was] advanced in large numbers, everywhere deploying into double and triple lines, overlapping our left for a third of a mile, pressing heavily upon our right, and overwhelming our center. It was evident Lee's whole army was approaching."

Then came the final blows that sent all remaining Union lines in full retreat. When Daniel's Brigade launched their final attack towards Sheads Woods on Oak Ridge, the rest of Rodes' Division attacked the ridge in concert. Union Brigadier General John Robinson personally ordered the 16th Maine to "hold" the 1st Corps' right flank "as long as there was a man left." Meanwhile, Major General William Pender's Division followed up the success of Brockenbrough and Pettigrew. Continuing the relentless attacks, Pender sent his fresh troops from McPherson's Ridge against a strong position of Union breastworks and artillery concentrated around the Seminary. Pender's men sustained heavy losses while charging across the open fields to the Seminary. They finally breached the Union defenses through a gap in the lines south of the breastworks. By this time, all Union troops from Barlow's Knoll to Oak Ridge and Seminary Ridge were retreating through town heading for the high ground of Cemetery Hill that lay to the south.

DESCRIPTION OF
    OR 1: 355 (Col. Wainwright's Artillery Report**)

FINAL STRIKE AGAINST OAK RIDGE
    OR 1: 290 (Gen. Robinson's Division Report)
    OR 1: 297-298 (Col. Batchelder's Report — 13th MA)
    OR 1: 301 (Col. Prey's Report — 104th NY)
    OR 2: 587 (Gen. Ramseur's Brigade Report**) — Read about Col. Battle.
    OR 2: 589-590 (Col. Grimes' Report** — 4th NC) — Claims the 4th NC were first Confederates to enter Gettysburg.
    OR 2: 590 (Maj. Lambeth's Report** — 14th NC)
    OR 2: 591 (Maj. Sillers' Report — 30th NC))
    OR 2: 592-593 (Col. O'Neal's Brigade Report)
    OR 2: 595 (Col. Battle's Report — 3rd AL)

FINAL STRIKE AGAINST SEMINARY RIDGE
    OR 1: 317-318, 321 (Col. Gates' Report — 20th NYS Militia / 80th NY)

OR 1: 328 (Col. McFarland's Report — 151st PA) — Read about McFarland's wounding and narrow escape with Private Wilson.
OR 1: 333 (Col. Wister's Report — Stone's Brigade) — Claim's Stone's Brigade resisted at the Seminary some time after 3:00 p.m. until "about 3:40 o'clock."
OR 1: 336 (Col. Dana's Report — Stone's Brigade)
OR 1: 343 (Col. Dwight's Report — 149th PA)
OR 1: 355-357 (Col. Wainwright's Artillery Report**)
OR 1: 360-361 (Lieut. Whittier's Report — Stevens' Battery)
OR 1: 362-363 (Lieut. Breck's Report — Reynolds' Battery)
OR 1: 364-365 (Capt. Cooper's Battery Report)
OR 2: 656-658 (Maj. Engelhard's Report** — Pender's Division)
OR 2: 661-662 (Col. Perrin's Brigade Report**)
OR 2: 669-670 (Gen. Scales' Brigade Report)
OR 2: 671 (Col. Lowrance's Report** — Scales' Brigade) — Only two field officers in brigade remained.

UNION RETREAT FROM OAK RIDGE AND SEMINARY RIDGE
OR 1: 251-253 (Gen. Doubleday's First Corps Report)
OR 1: 277 (Col. Rufus Dawe's Report — 6th WI)
OR 1: 283 (Gen. Cutler's Brigade Report)
OR 1: 292 (Col. Coulter's Report — 11th PA) — Retreated via the railroad cut.
OR 1: 295-296 (Col. Farnham's Report — 16th ME) — Reported 162 officers and men as "missing"! Most were presumably captured in the retreat.
OR 1: 321 (Col. Gates' Report — 20th NYS Militia / 80th NY) — Biddle's Brigade retreated via the railroad cut.
OR 1: 336 (Col. Dana's Report — Stone's Brigade) — Claims Stone's Brigade was the last to leave the field.
OR 1: 338-339 (Col. Musser's Report — 143rd PA)
OR 1: 356-357 (Col. Wainwright's Artillery Report**)
OR 1: 362-363 (Lieut. Breck's Report — Reynolds' Battery)
OR 1: 365 (Capt. Cooper's Battery Report)
OR 2: 554-555 (Gen. Rodes' Division Report) — "The enemy was thus routed at all points."

CONFEDERATES CAPTURE FEDERALS IN THE RAILROAD CUT
OR 2: 567 (Gen. Daniel's Brigade Report)
OR 2: 572 (Col. Brabble's Report — 32nd NC)
OR 2: 573 (Col. Lewis' Report — 43rd NC) — Claims brigade captured 500.
OR 2: 575 (Capt. Hopkins' Report — 45th NC) — His men found what was left of the 16th Maine's colors. "The remnants of what had been a fine Yankee flag were lying in different places."
OR 2: 578 (Capt. Van Brown's Report** — 2nd NC Battalion)

The Town of Gettysburg

The retreat of the Union 1st and 11th Corps was chaotic and confusing. Panicky and under enemy fire, many fleeing Federals found the town of Gettysburg to be a "gauntlet." Fences and pens became major obstacles while unfamiliar streets caused soldiers to get lost. The buildings, smoke, and incoming artillery fire made it difficult for troops to find their way south to the high ground. Large portions of regiments got separated from their commands and were left behind. Some, like the 17th Connecticut regiment, fought with ferocity but to no avail: "As we retreated, we loaded, halted, and poured destructive volleys into their ranks ... but we found the enemy too many for us. They poured in from every street in overwhelming numbers."

Major General Carl Schurz, in command of the 11th Corps, called several times for reinforcements to cover his retreat. From Cemetery Hill, Major General Oliver Howard eventually answered only after the 11th Corps line collapsed. He ordered Brigadier General Adolph Steinwehr to send Colonel Charles Coster's Brigade out to help slow the advancing Confederates so Union forces could reach Cemetery Hill, but it was too late. Coster's men, along with Captain Lewis Heckman's Battery, made a brave but hopeless stand against Confederates pouring in on them from the north and east. Many of them were captured, and Heckman lost two of his four guns.

Soon Lee's army was pouring into town from several directions. Ewell's Corps garnered the most prisoners. Early stressed the fact that his division captured "a very large number" of Federals and Rodes claimed his troops gathered "about 2,500 prisoners" alone. In fact, both Early and Rodes reported that they were "embarrassed" over just how many Union soldiers they easily captured. Those Federals that did escape consolidated on Cemetery Hill, and from there they could see a dire situation develop as evening approached. As one Union officer wrote, "...the whole town was surrounded and the enemy in possession of Gettysburg."

The Retreat Through Town
- OR 1: 253 (Gen. Doubleday's First Corps Report)
- OR 1: 277 (Col. Dawes' Report** — 6th WI)
- OR 1: 286 (Capt. Cook's Report — 76th NY) — Enemy fire made "falling bricks" a hazard in town.
- OR 1: 718 (Maj. Brady's Report** — 17th CT)
- OR 1: 735 (Col. Dobke's Report** — 45th NY)
- OR 1: 742 (Maj. Willis' Report — 119th NY)

Covering the Retreat
OR 1: 721 (Gen. Steinwehr's Division Report) — Read about Coster's Brigade.
OR 1: 748 (Maj. Osborn's Artillery Report) — Read about Heckman's Battery.
Confederates Capture Federals in Town
OR 1: 308 (Gen. Baxter's Brigade Report**) — Col. Wheelock of the 97th NY is captured, but escapes!
OR 1: 730 (Gen. Schurz's Division Report**) — Schimmelfennig in hiding.
OR 2: 469 (Gen. Early's Division Report**)
OR 2: 479 (Gen. Hays' Brigade Report)
OR 2: 555 (Gen. Rodes' Division Report**) — Captures 2,500 Union soldiers.
OR 2: 662 (Col. Perrin's Brigade Report**) — "The enemy completely routed and driven from every point, Gettysburg was now completely in our possession."

Cemetery Hill

"At 4:30 p.m., the [Union] columns reached Cemetery Hill, the enemy pressing hard," observed Major General Oliver Howard from its summit. Cemetery Hill was the highest ground immediately south of Gettysburg and named for the town graveyard atop its crest. It stood virtually treeless and from its heights Union officers could survey the entire field of battle and "command every eminence within easy range." Union Major Generals Reynolds, Howard, and Hancock commanded the field in sequence prior to Meade's arrival, and each recognized the hill's strategic importance. It had to be held if the Union army was to remain at Gettysburg and stand a chance against Lee's army.

Upon Reynolds' death, Howard was the ranking officer on the field and assumed command of all Union forces. Meade, who was at Taneytown, Maryland, sent Hancock (junior in rank to Howard) to assume command in his place. When Hancock reached Gettysburg between 4:00 and 4:30 p.m., he and Howard disagreed over who was in command, but they worked together to rally the retreating troops coming through town and concentrate them on and around Cemetery Hill. The Baltimore Pike was the main thoroughfare south out of Gettysburg from which many troops arrived, and it ran directly over Cemetery Hill. Howard arranged troops and batteries on the hill's portion east of the pike, and Hancock did the same for the west side. When Confederates reached the south end of town, Union troops were getting into position all around Cemetery Hill and more than 40 guns stood atop its summit.

Lee saw the importance of Cemetery Hill too. His Second Corps General, Richard "Dick" Ewell, reported that on "entering the town I received a message from the commanding general [Lee] to attack this hill, if I could do so to advantage." Ewell's divisions under Early and Rodes were to bear the brunt of the attack, but Early and Rodes were split over its advantage. Early urged "an immediate advance upon the enemy ... in order to get possession of the hills to which he had fallen back." But in contrast, Rodes observed that the Federals "displayed quite a formidable line of infantry and artillery" on Cemetery Hill and, coupled with his division's losses that day, "to have attacked this line... would have been absurd." When Ewell sent for support from A. P. Hill, Hill claimed his troops were exhausted and disordered and that he was "content" to halt any further attack out of fear his men would "encounter fresh troops of the enemy." Then Ewell made his decision. O'Neal's and Doles' brigades were already in the act of charging Cemetery Hill when they were suddenly recalled. "I could not bring artillery to bear on [Cemetery Hill], and all the troops with me were jaded by twelve hours' marching and fighting...," reported Ewell. He ordered no further Confederate attack, and there ended the first day of battle.

DESCRIPTION OF
OR 1: 702 (Gen. Howard's XI Corps Report)
OR 1: 727 (Gen. Schurz's Division Report) — Schurz observed First Corps fighting on Seminary Ridge from this hill.
OR 1: 722 (Gen. Steinwehr's Division Report)
OR 1: 724 (Col. Smith's Brigade Report) — The openness of this hill would make it easy for Confederate sharpshooters to kill Union soldiers on the hill.
OR 2: 480 (Gen. Hays' Brigade Report)
OR 2: 597-598 (Maj. Blackford's Report**) — Blackford's "Corps of Sharpshooters" occupied houses from which they fired on the Union lines.

FEDERAL DECISION TO USE THE HILL
OR 1: 72 (Gen. Meade's Dispatch) — "I immediately sent up General Hancock to assume command."
OR 1: 252 (Gen. Doubleday's I Corps Report**) — He received confusing orders from Hancock and Howard.
OR 1: 368 (Gen. Hancock's II Corps Report)
OR 1: 702-704 (Gen. Howard's XI Corps Report)
OR 1: 924-925 (Gen. Buford's Dispatch) — "there seems to be no directing person"

IMPORTANCE OF THE HILL
OR 1: 725 (Col. Smith's Brigade Report)
OR 1: 721 (Gen. Steinwehr's Division Report) — "Cemetery Hill is the commanding point of the whole position..."
OR 1: 735 (Col. Dobke's Report — 45th NY)

Fortifying the Hill with Union Guns

OR 1: 361 (Lieut. Whittier's Report — Stevens' Battery) — This battery was positioned on Stevens' Knoll for which the knoll is named.

OR 1: 749 (Major Osborn's Artillery Report) — There were 52 guns on Cemetery Hill by July 2. Osborn's artillery "commanded ... every point" from the hill.

OR 1: 891 (Capt. Taft's Battery Report**)

OR 1: 892-893 (Capt. Edgell's Battery Report**)

OR 1: 893-894 (Lieut. Norton's Battery Report)

OR 1: 894 (Capt. Rickett's Battery Report**)

Ewell's Decision Not to Attack the Hill

OR 2: 445-446 (Gen. Ewell's II Corps Report)

OR 2: 456 (Col. Brown's Artillery Report) — Brown hoped to take Culp's Hill.

OR 2: 469-470 (Gen. Early's Division Report)

OR 2: 555 (Gen. Rodes' Division Report**) — Excellent explanation for not attacking. Rodes' explanation clearly defends Ewell's decision.

OR 2: 593 (Col. O'Neal's Brigade Report**) — O'Neal claims that his and Doles' brigade were in the act of charging Cemetery Hill when they were recalled.

OR 2: 607 (Gen. Hill's III Corps Report**) — Hill defends Ewell's decision.

3

The Second Day

"...the cemetery commanded every eminence within easy range...."

The Evergreen Cemetery Gatehouse stood atop Cemetery Hill just south of town. The hill served as the anchoring position around which the Union army formed its famous fishhook position by July 2, 1863. More Union guns fortified the hill than anywhere else because of its strategic value, and taking it became a key objective in General Lee's plan of attack. This chapter provides the battle reports and parts of those reports that discuss the Confederate attacks against the Union army on the second day. Included herein are the fighting at Devil's Den, Little Round Top, the Wheatfield, Peach Orchard, Cemetery Ridge, Cemetery Hill, and Culp's Hill.

Cemetery, Seminary & Warfield Ridges

In the night and early morning of July 2, both armies continued to concentrate around Gettysburg. General Meade, who reached town near midnight, formed his arriving troops around Cemetery Hill where the 1st and 11th Corps had regrouped. To the right on Culp's Hill went Slocum's 12th Corps, to the immediate left along the northern half of Cemetery Ridge went Hancock's 2nd Corps. Sickles' 3rd Corps continued the line down to the Round Tops. The entire Union line, from the Round Tops to Culp's Hill, stretched about two-and-a-half miles and formed the shape of a fishhook. This position gave Meade the advantage of interior lines from which to maneuver.

By the afternoon, Lee's army mirrored the Union line in a similar but much longer fishhook shape, stretching seven miles from north of Culp's Hill through town and south along Seminary Ridge down to Warfield Ridge (the southern end of Seminary Ridge). The three corps of Lee's army were positioned as follows: "General Ewell occupied the left of [the] line, General Hill the center, and General Longstreet [on] the right." To dislodge the Union army from its position, Lee wanted a coordinated attack from all three of his corps. Longstreet was to attack Meade's left, Ewell was to strike Meade's right, and Hill was "to threaten the center of the Federal line in order to prevent re-enforcements [sic] being sent to either wing." The main assault would come from Longstreet, but his troops were the last to arrive on the field. In his approach, he had spent the morning and afternoon marching and countermarching his men in an attempt to remain undetected as he got them into position "opposite the enemy's left about 4 p.m."

Meanwhile, Union Major General Dan Sickles had become unsettled with the position of his 3rd Corps along south Cemetery Ridge and wanted to move to higher ground in his front. He had given permission to Colonel Hiram Berdan to lead a reconnaissance to some woods on Seminary Ridge "with directions to feel the enemy, and to discover their movements." When Berdan's men were "driven back by overwhelming numbers" of Confederates arriving on Lee's right Sickles subsequently ordered his line forward "to meet the attack." It was about 2:00 p.m. whe he advanced his corps, forming a salient at the Peach Orchard with his right along the Emmitsburg Road and his left extending through the Wheatfield to Devil's Den. Sickles' line was stretched and fragmented over more than a mile, thin in places and having gaps in others, and he had left the Round Tops unoccupied. Moreover, the 3rd Corps was a half-mile from the rest of Meade's line, which went against Meade's original orders to Sickles. When Meade rode out to inspect Sickles' line, he found it "too far in advance" and wanted it withdrawn, but it was too late because Longstreet's attack was in motion.

It was around 4:00 p.m. when Longstreet's artillery opened fire on Sickles' line and General John Bell Hood's Division "moved to the attack." The attack was made against the Union left "en echelon," one division at a time. Hood's Division occupied Longstreet's extreme right on Warfield Ridge and marched out in the direction of Big Round Top and Devil's Den. Hood's troops marched a half-mile across open fields and over fences while under considerable artillery fire. Shortly into the advance, Hood was struck in the left arm by a shell fragment and had to be carried from the field. His wound was severe and it rendered his arm permanently useless. Major General Lafayette McLaws Division advanced next, followed by Major General Richard Anderson's Division of Hill's Corps. As the Confederate assault struck Sickles' advanced line, the course of battle progressed north from the Devil's Den and Little Round Top, to the Wheatfield, the Peach Orchard, and Cemetery Ridge.

Late in the afternoon, Major General J. E. B. Stuart finally arrived with his cavalry division. Around 2:00 a.m. that morning he had left Carlisle after burning the U.S. Cavalry barracks there. Along the way to Gettysburg, he encountered Federal cavalry at Hunterstown in the early afternoon. A skirmish ensued, principally between brigades of Confederate Brigadier General Wade Hampton and Union Brigadier General George Custer. The fight was brief and ended in a stalemate with few casualties. After Stuart reached Gettysburg, he positioned his cavalry in rear of Ewell's Corps on the York and Heidlersburg roads to guard the left wing of Lee's army.

Lee's Plan of Attack
OR 2: 308, 318 (Gen. Lee's Report)
OR 2: 358 (Gen. Longstreet's I Corps Report)
OR 2: 446 (Gen. Ewell's II Corps Report)
OR 2: 608 (Gen. Hill's III Corps Report)

Reconnaissance by Berdan's Sharpshooters
OR 1: 482 (Gen. Birney's Division Report)
OR 1: 493 (Gen. Ward's Brigade Report)
OR 1: 507 (Col. Lakeman's Report — 3rd ME)
OR 1: 515 (Col. Berdan's Report — U.S. Shartshooters)
OR 1: 516-517 (Col. Trepp — 1st U.S. Sharpshooters)
OR 1: 939 (Col. Devin's Brigade Report)
OR 2: 350 (Gen. Pendleton's Artillery Report)
OR 2: 613-614 (Gen. Anderson's Division Report)

OR 2: 617 (Gen. Wilcox's Brigade Report**) — The 10th Alabama fought Berdan's men in the woods on Seminary Ridge.

SICKLES ADVANCES HIS CORPS
OR 1: 130-132 (Historicus**)
OR 1: 370 (Gen. Hancock's II Corps Report)
OR 1: 483 (Gen. Birney's Division Report**)
OR 1: 532 (Gen. Humphreys' Division Report)
OR 1: 556 (Maj. Bodine's Report — 26th PA) — This regiment was "detailed to clear away fences in front ... to facilitate the movement of our troops."
OR 1: 565-566 (Col. Austin's Report — 72nd NY) — Sickles' advance began at 2:00 p.m.
OR 1: 581-582 (Capt. Randolph's Artillery Report**) — Explains why Sickles advanced.
OR 1: 590 (Lieut. Freeborn's Report** — Bucklyn's Battery) — Explains the problem with Sickles' line.

LONGSTREET'S COUNTERMARCH AND ARRIVAL ON SEMINARY RIDGE
OR 1: 483 (Gen. Birney's Division Report) — Claims he had Smith's and Clark's batteries fire on Confederates "moving to our left" into position at 3:30 p.m.
OR 2: 358 (Gen. Longstreet's 1st Corps Report**)
OR 2: 366-367 (Gen. Kershaw's Brigade Report)
OR 2: 391 (Col. Scruggs' Report — 4th AL) — Marched 24 miles and arrived at 3: 30 p.m.
OR 2: 395 (Col. Sheffield's Report — 48th AL) — Marched 20 miles.
OR 2: 396 (Col. White's Report — Anderson's Brigade) — Noted the "broiling sun."
OR 2: 401 (Maj. McDaniel's Report — 11th GA) — Noted the "burning sun."
OR 2: 420 (Col. Shepherd's Report — 2nd GA) — Longstreet's "circuitous" march began at 1:00 p.m. and noted the "extreme heat."
OR 2: 424 (Col. Hodges' Report — 17th GA) — Longstreet's "circuitous route" and the "excessive heat."
OR 2: 425 (Col. Waddell's Report — 20th GA) — Got into position while under Union artillery fire.
OR 2: 617-618 (Gen. Wilcox's Brigade Report**)

CONFEDERATE GUNS OPEN THE ATTACKS
OR 1: 483 (Gen. Birney's Division Report)
OR 1: 587 (Capt. Winslow's Battery Report)
OR 1: 588 (Capt. Smith's Battery Report)
OR 1: 749 (Maj. Osborn's Artillery Report) — Confederates guns fire on entire Union line.
OR 2: 319 (Gen. Lee's Report) — Longstreet's batteries opened at 4 p.m.
OR 2: 351 (Gen. Pendleton's Artillery Report)

OR 2: 470 (Gen. Early's Division Report) — Confederate guns on the army's left & right open fire at 4 p.m.

Longstreet's Delayed Infantry Assault Begins

OR 1: 483 (Gen. Birney's Division Report)

OR 1: 498 (Maj. Danks' Report — 63rd PA) — Claims the assault began between 3:00 and 4:00 p.m.

OR 1: 583 (Capt. Randolph's Artillery Report**) — Claims the infantry attack began "shortly after 3 p.m."

OR 2: 319 (Gen. Lee's Report)

OR 2: 359 (Gen. Longstreet's I Corps Report) — General Hood's wounding.

OR 2: 367-368 (Gen. Kershaw's Brigade Report**) — Kershaw's report is amazingly descriptive of the Peach Orchard, Rose Farm, Wheatfield, Round Top, and woods and fields.

OR 2: 372 (Maj. Maffett's Report — 3rd SC) — Claims the attack commenced at 4:00 p.m.

OR 2: 391 (Col. Scruggs' Report — 4th AL) — Marched half-mile under enemy artillery fire.

OR 2: 395 (Col. Sheffield's Report — 48th AL) — Advanced 1 mile over "the worst cliffs of rocks."

OR 2: 401 (Maj. McDaniel's Report — 11th GA) — Advanced 1 mile under terrific enemy artillery fire.

OR 2: 403 (Maj. Gee's Report — 59th GA) — "Double-quicked ... 400 yards under a severe shelling and a scorching sun" that exhausted them going into the attack.

OR 2: 404 (Gen. Robertson's Brigade Report) — Began advance within minutes of arriving on Seminary Ridge.

OR 2: 408 (Col. Work's Report — 1st TX) — Advanced at 4 p.m. for a half-mile.

OR 2: 410-411 (Maj. Bane's Report — 4th TX) — Double-quicked across fields.

OR 2: 414 (Gen. Benning's Brigade Report)

OR 2: 426 (Col. Waddell's Report — 20th GA) — Advanced at 5 p.m.

OR 2. 608 (Gen. Hill's III Corps Report) — General Anderson's brigades are to advance "en echelon," and General Pender is mortally wounded.

OR 2: 614 (Gen. Anderson's Division Report**) — "I was ... ordered to put the troops of my division into action by brigades [after] those of General Longstreet's ...".

OR 2: 618 (Gen. Wilcox's Brigade Report)

OR 2: 622 (Gen. Wright's Brigade Report)

OR 2: 631 (Col. Lang's Brigade Report) — Advanced at 6 p.m.

OR 2: 633 (Gen. Posey's Brigade Report)

OR 2: 658-659 (Maj. Engelhard's Report — Pender's Division) — General Pender's mortal wounding.

DISMANTLING BURLING'S "NEW JERSEY" BRIGADE TO REINFORCE SICKLES
OR 1: 571 (Col. Burling's Brigade Report) — "My command being now all taken from me...".
OR 1: 574 (Col. Bailey's Report — 2nd NH) — Sent to the Peach Orchard.
OR 1: 575-576 (Col. Sewell's Report — 5th NJ) — Sent to the Emmitsburg Road.
OR 1: 577 (Col. Gilkyson's Report — 6th NJ) — Sent to the Devil's Den.
OR 1: 578-579 (Maj. Cooper's Report — 7th NJ) — Sent to the Peach Orchard.

CAVALRY SKIRMISH AT HUNTERSTOWN AND J. E. B. STUART'S LATE ARRIVAL
OR 1: 914 (Gen. Pleasonton's Cavalry Corps Report)
OR 1: 992 (Gen. Kilpatrick's Division Report)
OR 1: 998 (Gen. Custer's Brigade Report)
OR 2: 321-322 (Gen. Lee's Report**)
OR 2: 495 (Col. Jones' Battalion Report)
OR 2: 497 (Capt. Green's Battery Report)
OR 2: 697, 708-709 (Gen. Stuart's Division Report**) — Stuart defends his absence from Lee on pp. 708-709.
OR 2: 724 (Gen. Hampton's Brigade Report)

Devil's Den and the Slaughter Pen

No officer called it "Devil's Den," but many who fought there described the place. Its immense rocks were unlike anything the soldiers had ever seen, and they provided great cover to anyone who held them. Devil's Den, at the south end of Houck's Ridge, was barren of trees while the northern half of the ridge was covered by woods of the Rose Farm. To its west lay a triangular field enclosed by three stone walls. To its east, between the Den and Little Round Top, was the Plum Run valley that Confederates called "the ravine." From there Plum Run runs south through a narrow, heavily-bouldered passage between the Den and Big Round Top that officers called "the gorge."

Only one of Sickles' brigades, commanded by Brigadier General Hobart Ward, and one battery, under Captain James Smith, occupied Devil's Den and Houck's Ridge, holding "the extreme left of the [Union] army." They were all that stood between the Round Tops and Hood's advancing Confederates. As Ward put it, "we had but a single line of battle to receive the shock" of Hood's attack. Smith "opened on the advancing enemy" with four of his guns posted atop the crest of Devil's Den, but Ward's "line awaited the clash" as the Rebels came on "en masse, yelling and shouting." The 1st Texas and 3rd Arkansas of Brigadier General Jerome Robertson's Brigade attacked through the Rose Woods and the triangular field. When they got within 200 yards, Ward's Brigade opened fire. The Southerners in the Rose Woods were halted by three of Ward's regiments including the 20th Indiana who lost their commander, Colonel John Wheeler, and by the 17th Maine firing from edge of the Wheatfield bordering the woods. Meanwhile, across the triangular field, the 1st Texas fought against Smith's battery and the 124th New York. There "for the space of one and half hours," recalled Ward, "did we advance and retire, both parties endeavoring to gain possession of the [Triangular Field]." When the Confederates attacked a second time, the Texans nearly captured Smith's guns, but Colonel Augustus Van Horn Ellis led his 124th New Yorkers in a dramatic countercharge. They repelled the attack, but a new Confederate line struck them and Ellis was "shot through the head." It was Brigadier General Henry Benning's Brigade of Georgians, and their arrival changed the course of the fight.

At the same time, Colonel Elijah Walker's 4th Maine infantry was protecting Smith's Battery from the 44th and 48th Alabama regiments of Brigadier General Evander Law's Brigade advancing from the gorge. But when troops of the 44th got within the rocks of Devil's Den and fired on Smith's gunners from the left, Benning's and Robertson's men assaulted the battery from the front. Smith had to withdraw his crews, but the 4th Maine charged to the crest to save the guns. The 99th Pennsylvania joined the Mainers in fighting back the Confederates who had reached the battery, but even together they could not hold the guns for long. On the crest above Devil's Den, three of Smith's guns were abandoned.

"The enemy now concentrated his force on our extreme left, with the intention to turn our left flank through [the] gorge ...," wrote Ward. Some of Benning's Georgians charged into the gorge and joined the Alabamans already there. But "when the right of [my] brigade reached the gorge," recalled Benning, "[we endured a] terrible fire from [two guns] which swept down the gorge." This was Smith's rear section placed in the valley and used to hold off the Confederates in the gorge until Federal reinforcements arrived. Shortly, the 40th New York and the 6th New Jersey came from the Wheatfield and "marched down the gully" of Plum Run in front of his guns, all the way "fighting like tigers." The 40th New York charged several times into the gorge to stop the Rebel advance, but these repeated strikes only stalled them. With Benning's Brigade on the scene, Confederates well outnumbered Ward's men, compelling them to retreat. Ward's regiments withdrew from right to left off Houck's Ridge under close enemy fire. Many of the 4th Maine and 99th Pennsylvania were captured since they were the last to pull out. As Confederates seized Houck's Ridge and captured Smith's guns atop Devil's Den, the 40th New York too was forced to retire. Some of the Yankees fled to the Little Round Top but most withdrew up Plum Run valley. The 6th New Jersey covered their retreat. When General Benning surveyed the scene, he observed that "dead and wounded lay scattered over the [entire] ground of the conflict and of the retreat." The scene was so ghastly in the gorge that it would be called the "Slaughter Pen."

Description of
- OR 1: 483 (Gen. Birney's Division Report) — Mentions "the gorge".
- OR 1: 493-494 Gen. Ward's Brigade Report) — Refers to "rocky eminence" and "gorge" to describe this landscape.
- OR 1: 513 (Maj. Moore's Report — 99th PA)
- OR 1: 526 (Col. Egan's Report — 40th NY) — Uses "ravine" to describe Plum Run Valley between Houck's Ridge and the Round Tops.
- OR 1: 582 (Maj. Randolph's Artillery Report) — The "rocky hill" rendered horses useless.
- OR 1: 588 (Capt. Smith's Battery Report) — Mentions the "Devil's Cave".
- OR 1: 592 (Gen. Sykes' V Corps Report)
- OR 2: 393-394 (Col. Perry's Report — 44th AL)
- OR 2: 404-405 (Gen. Robertson's Brigade Report) — His reference to "the hill" refers to Houck's Ridge.
- OR 2: 414 (Gen. Benning's Brigade Report) — Benning's description of an "oblong mountain peak, or spur" refers to Devil's Den where the "enemy's first line of battle" was positioned. He uses "gorge" to refer to the narrow passage between "the peak" (Devil's Den ridge) and "the mountain" (Big & Little Round Top, which Benning saw as one mountain) that opens into Plum Run Valley.
- OR 2: 420 (Col. Shepherd's Report — 2nd GA) — Mentions "a rocky eminence".
- OR 2: 421 (Col. DuBose's Report — 15th GA) — Refers to Houck's Ridge as "a high, wooded, rocky hill".
- OR 2: 425 (Col. Hodges' Report — 17th GA) — Mentions "a deep gorge".
- OR 2: 426 (Col. Waddell's Report — 20th GA) — Describes the Devil's Den area as "a steep, rocky, rugged hill".

Robertson's Confederates Attack Houck's Ridge and Devil's Den
- OR 1: 493 (Gen. Ward's Brigade Report)
- OR 1: 506 (Col. Taylor's Report — 20th IN)
- OR 1: 511 (Col. Higgins' Report — 86th NY)
- OR 1: 512 (Col. Cummins' Report — 124th NY)
- OR 1: 513 (Maj. Moore's Report — 99th PA)
- OR 1: 520 (Col. DeTrobriand's Brigade Report)
- OR 1: 588 (Capt. Smith's Battery Report)
- OR 2: 404-405 (Gen. Robertson's Brigade Report**)

OR 2: 407 (Col. Manning's Report — 3rd AR)
OR 2: 408 (Col. Work's Report — 1st TX)

Law's Confederates Attack the Gorge and Devil's Den
OR 1: 509-510 (Adjutant Sawyer's Report — 4th Maine)
OR 1: 518-519 (Maj. Stoughton's Report — 2nd U.S. Sharpshooters)
OR 1: 588 (Capt. Smith's Battery Report)
OR 2: 393-394 (Col. Perry's Report** — 44th AL)
OR 2: 395-396 (Col. Sheffield's Report — 48th AL)

The Fight for Smith's Guns
OR 1: 510 (Adjutant Sawyer's Report — 4th ME)
OR 1: 513 (Maj. Moore's Report) — 99th PA)
OR 1: 582-583 (Maj. Randolph's Artillery Report) — Smith's battery loses three guns.
OR 1: 588-589 (Capt. Smith's Battery Report) — 4th Maine comes to Smith's aid.
OR 2: 393-394 (Col. Perry's Report — 44th AL)
OR 2: 405 (Gen. Robertson's Brigade Report) — Claims 1st Texas captured Smith's guns twice.
OR 2: 409 (Col. Work's Report** — 1st TX) — Read about Private Barbee, and about the mangling of dead from Union artillery directed at the Den.
OR 2: 414-415, 416 (Gen. Benning's Brigade Report**)
OR 2: 421-422 (Col. Dubose's Report** — 15th GA)
OR 2: 424-425 (Col. Hodges' Report — 17th GA)
OR 2: 425-426 (Col. Waddell's Report** — 20th GA)

Georgians & Alabamans Push Through the Gorge
OR 1: 494 (Gen. Ward's Brigade Report**)
OR 1: 520 (Col. DeTrobriand's Brigade Report)
OR 1: 526 (Col. Egan's Report — 40th NY)
OR 1: 577 (Col. Gilkyson's Report — 6th NJ)
OR 1: 582-583 (Maj. Randolph's Artillery Report) — Smith's two reserve guns.
OR 1: 589 (Capt. Smith's Battery Report)
OR 2: 394 (Col. Perry's Report — 44th AL)
OR 2: 414 (Gen. Benning's Brigade Report)
OR 2: 420 (Col. Shepperd's Report — 2nd GA)
OR 2: 425 (Col. Hodges' Report — 17th GA)

The Federals Flee and the Confederates Settle In
OR 1: 506 (Col. Taylor's Report — 20th IN)
OR 1: 513 (Maj. Moore's Report — 99th PA)
OR 1: 526-527 (Col. Egan's Report — 40th NY)
OR 1: 577-578 (Col. Gilkyson's Report — 6th NJ)
OR 1: 589 (Capt. Smith's Battery Report)
OR 2: 406 (Gen. Robertson's Brigade Report**)

OR 2: 409 (Col Work's Report** — 1st TX) — Read about Private Barbee.
OR 2: 415-416 (Gen. Benning's Brigade Report**)
OR 2: 426 (Col. Waddell's Report** — 20th GA)

Little Round Top and the Valley of Death

Little Round Top stood at the south end of the Union line. Union officers called it by other various names — "Sugar Loaf," "Rock Hill," or "Granite Spur" — while Confederate officers referred to it simply as "the mountain." Its east slope was covered by woods, but its summit and west slope had been cleared of trees and were strewn with rocks and boulders. Adjacent Big Round Top, known better as just "Round Top," was taller but completely wooded which negated any firing advantage to whomever held it. Instead, Little Round Top was the highest ground on the battlefield from which to observe and fire on the enemy, and the Union army secured it in the nick of time. In the words of one Confederate officer whose attacking troops reached its base as Federals occupied its slopes and summit on July 2nd, "we found [it] to be the strongest natural position I ever saw."

Several heroes helped save Little Round Top for the Union army that day. The first was Major General Gouverner Warren, Meade's chief topographical engineer. As Meade rode out to meet Sickles near the Peach Orchard in the midafternoon, Warren rode to Little Round Top and found it abandoned except for a few signalmen. He recognized that if the hill fell into Confederate hands, the Union line along Cemetery Ridge would have to be abandoned. Warren also discovered that Confederates had massed south of the Emmitsburg Road and outflanked Sickles' line. He immediately requested troops to the summit. These Federal soldiers arrived just before the Confederate attack reached the hill. His foresight and quick actions later earned him the sobriquet of "Savior of Little Round Top."

The first to respond to Warren's call was Colonel Strong Vincent's Brigade. He positioned his four regiments on the south slope of Little Round Top. The 20th Maine "occupied the extreme left of the brigade" facing Big Round Top while the 16th Michigan was on a "ledge of rocks" on the right overlooking Devil's Den. Vincent told Colonel Joshua Chamberlain, commander of the 20th Maine, that his men now held "the extreme left of our general line" and that they were to "hold that ground at all hazards." Chamberlain immediately sent out Company B under Captain Walter Morrill to watch for movement against the regiment's left flank, and they took position near a stone wall in the woods to his left.

Vincent's entire brigade fronted the saddle between the Round Tops which would become the real "Valley of Death." According to Colonel James Rice of the 44th New York, "The brigade had scarcely formed line of battle and pushed forward its skirmishers when ... the enemy's forces, under General Hood, made a desperate attack [here]." The attackers were four regiments from Law's and Robertson's brigades — the 48th Alabama, 4th and 5th Texas, and 4th Alabama. This group had passed to the right of Devil's Den and came over the north slope of Big Round Top, through its woods, and attacked into the saddle and up the bouldered south slope of Little Round Top. They assaulted the center and right of Vincent's Brigade twice. Meanwhile, Colonel William Oates led the 47th and 15th Alabama "on the extreme right" of the Confederate attack over the upper north slope and crest of Big Round Top. They struck the left half of Vincent's line, eventually concentrating against Colonel Joshua Chamberlain's 20th Maine as the 4th and 5th Texas led a third and final assault against Vincent's right.

The last assault on Vincent's right was nearly successful when part of the 16th Michigan fell back. Vincent quickly rallied the men, but fell mortally wounded. He died five days later and was posthumously promoted to brigadier general. To help save this position, Warren had ordered Brigadier General Stephen Weed's Brigade to the support of Vincent's men. The lead regiment was the 140th New York, commanded by Colonel Patrick O'Rorke. He rushed his men up the east slope of Little Round Top and upon reaching the crest, O'Rorke continued leading his New Yorkers on a heroic charge down the opposite slope to reinforce the 16th Michigan. O'Rorke was killed almost immediately but he got his men there in time to repel the Texans. Coming up behind O'Rorke was Lieutenant Charles Hazlett's Battery and the remaining regiments of Weed's Brigade. Hazlett's men placed six guns on the rocky crest. Shortly after the guns had begun firing, General Weed "was mortally wounded on the summit near the battery ... [just] a few moments after [he] had placed his [brigade] in position." He called for Hazlett, who came and knelt beside him, but "while offering his assistance to General Weed, [he too] fell, mortally wounded" with a Confederate minie ball to the brain. Weed died later that night. Hazlett's guns continued to pour "a terrific fire of artillery" into the Confederates on Devil's Den and Houck's Ridge. Colonel Work of the 1st Texas claimed many of his men were brutally killed by it, "some losing their heads, and others so horribly mutilated that their identity could scarcely be established."

Meanwhile, the fighting raged between Oates and Chamberlain. At one point, Chamberlain saw some of Oates' men maneuvering behind their line to their far right in an attempt to outflank the 20th Maine. Chamberlain recalled that upon seeing this movement, "I immediately stretched my regiment to the left ... and at the same time 'refusing' my left wing, so that it was nearly at right angles with my right." This thinned his front to only a single rank in places. "But we were not a moment too soon," claimed Chamberlain, "the enemy's flanking column ... burst upon my left." For about an hour they pushed each other's lines up and down the slope, often coming within about "10 paces" or "a dozen yards"of each other. At times some of Oates' men broke through the 20th Maine's line "in several places, and the fight was literally hand to hand." Chamberlain claimed his men withstood four assaults, while Oates claimed his men withstood five. Running low on ammunition and unable to take another assault, Chamberlain remembered, "My men were firing their last shot and getting ready to 'club' their muskets. It was imperative to strike before we were struck… At that crisis, I ordered the bayonet. The word was enough. It ran like fire along the line, from man to man, and rose into a shout, with which they sprang forward upon the enemy…." The left wing of the 20th Maine made a "right wheel" forward until coming in line with the right wing and the entire regiment continued, all the while sweeping the surprised enemy in their front. From behind the stone wall in the woods to the left, Captain Morrill's Company B rejoined the 20th in the attack, further surprising the Confederates on their flank as they were struck by Chamberlain's charge. In this maneuver, the 20th Maine captured many prisoners, mostly of the 15th and 47th Alabama. To save his command from total destruction, Oates had "ordered a retreat" and he and the rest of his men fled back over Round Top. The battle for Little Round Top had raged for three hours. As "night closed the fight [there]," wrote Union Major General George Sykes, "the key of the battle-field was in our possession intact."

DESCRIPTION OF PLACE AND NICKNAMES
    OR 1: 381 (Col. McKeen's Report — Cross' Brigade) — "Sugar Loaf Hill"
    OR 1: 482 (Gen. Birney's Division Report) — "Sugar Loaf Hill"
    OR 1: 493 (Gen. Ward's Brigade Report) — "Round Top or Sugar Loaf Hill"
    OR 1: 592-593 (Gen. Sykes' V Corps Report) — Refers to Plum Run Valley as "the gorge".
    OR 1: 602 (Gen. Barnes' Division Report) — "Little Round Top"
    OR 1: 617-619 (Col. Rice's Report — Vincent's Brigade) — Claims Big Round Top is known as "Round Top hill" or just "Round Top".
    OR 1: 623 (Col. Chamberlain's Report — 20th ME) — Refers to Little Round Top as "Granite Spur" and Big Round Top as "Sugar Loaf".

OR 1: 630 (Lieut. Conner's Report — 44th NY) — "Round Top hill"
OR 1: 634 (Gen. Ayres' Division Report) — "Round Top hill"
OR 1: 647 (Capt. Hancock's Report — 7th U.S.) — "Rock Hill"
OR 1: 649 (Maj. Floyd-Jones' Report — 11th U.S.) — "Sugar Loaf or Round Top Mountain"
OR 1: 651 (Col. Garrard's Report — Weed's Brigade) — "Round Top ridge"
OR 1: 653 (Gen. Crawford's Division Report) — Refers to Little Round Top as "a rocky ridge" and Big Round Top as "Round Top".
OR 1: 658 (Col. Fisher's Brigade Report) — Claims Big Round Top is just called "Round Top".
OR 1: 659 (Capt. Martin's Artillery Report) — "Rock Hill"
OR 1: 662 (Capt. Gibb's Battery Report) — "Weed's Hill"
OR 1: 855 (Gen. Greene's Brigade Report) — "Sugar Loaf Mountain"
OR 2: 367 & 369 (Gen. Kershaw's Brigade Report) — "the mountain"
OR 2: 393-394 (Col. Perry's Report — 44th AL) — "the mountain"
OR 2: 399 (Capt. Hillyer's Report — 9th GA) — "the mountain"
OR 2: 404 (Gen. Robertson's Brigade Report) — "the mountain"
OR 2: 411 (Maj. Bane's Report — 4th TX) — "the mountain"

Importance of Little Round Top
OR 1: 617 (Col. Rice's Report — Vincent's Brigade)
OR 1: 825 (Gen. Geary's Division Report)

Warren's Discovery
OR 1: 593 (Gen. Sykes' V Corps Report) — Claims Warren positioned Vincent's brigade.
OR 1: 600 (Gen. Barnes' Division Report)
OR 1: 651 (Col. Garrard's Report — Weed's Brigade)

The Confederate Attack Over Round Top
OR 1: 515 (Col. Berdan's Report — U.S. Sharpshooters)
OR 1: 518-519 (Maj. Stoughton's Report — 2nd U.S. Sharpshooters) — His troops try to stall the Confederate advance over Big Round Top.
OR 2: 391 (Col. Scruggs' Report — 4th AL)
OR 2: 392 (Col. Oates' Report — 15th AL)
OR 2: 395 (Maj. Campbell's Report — 47th AL) — The commanding colonel remained too far behind!
OR 2: 395-396 (Col. Sheffield's Report -- 48th AL)
OR 2: 405-406 (Gen. Robertson's Brigade Report**)
OR 2: 411 (Maj. Bane's Report** — 4th TX)
OR 2: 412 (Col. Bryan's Report** — 5thTX)
OR 2: 413 (Maj. Rogers' Report** -- 5th TX) — Charged three times.

Vincent's Brigade to the Rescue
OR 1: 592-593 (Gen. Sykes' V Corps Report**)

OR 1: 602-603, 604 (Gen. Barnes' Division Report**) — Read of Vincent's promotion and death on p. 604.
OR 1: 616-617 (Col. Rice's Report** — Vincent's Brigade) — See map on p. 619.
OR 1: 620 (Adj. Herendeen's General Orders No. 5**) — Vincent died July 7th.
OR 1: 622-623 (Col. Chamberlain's Report** — 20th ME)
OR 1: 628 (Col. Welch's Report — 16th MI) — Claims brigade got into position at 4 p.m. "under heavy fire," and later mentions confusion over orders causing some to leave the line.
OR 1: 630 (Col. Conner's Report** — 44th NY) — Describes how and when the fighting began.
OR 1: 632 (Capt. Woodward's Report — 83rd PA) — Fighting lasted three hours.
OR 1: 1041 (Gen. Meade's Letter**) — Recommendation of promotion of Colonel Strong Vincent to rank of Brigadier General.

O'RORKE, HAZLETT, AND WEED
OR 1: 593 (Gen. Sykes' V Corps Report)
OR 1: 617 (Col. Rice's Report) — Mentions O'Rorke's 140th New York.
OR 1: 624 (Col. Chamberlain's Report — 20th ME)
OR 1: 651-652 (Col. Garrard's Report** — Weed's Brigade) — Garrard claims Hazlett followed O'Rorke up Little Round Top, and that Weed's brigade deployed down the slope of Little Round Top until being pushed back.
OR 1: 659-660 (Capt. Martin's Artillery Report) — Hazlett's battery and death.
OR 1: 662 (Capt. Gibb's Battery Report**) — Gibbs' guns fired as Confederates pushed Weed's brigade back up the slopes of Little Round Top.

CHAMBERLAIN'S DEFENSE
OR 1: 603 (Gen. Barnes' Division Report**)
OR 1: 617 (Col. Rice's Report — Vincent's Brigade) — See map on p. 619.
OR 1: 623-625 (Col. Chamberlain's Report** — 20th ME)
OR 2: 392-393 (Col. Oates' Report** — 15th AL)

CONSTRUCTING UNION BREASTWORKS AND STONE WALLS
OR 2: 416 (Gen. Benning's Brigade Report**) — "The enemy employed the whole night in throwing up two lines of breastworks ... The sound of the stones dropping into place could be distinctly heard from our line during the whole night."
OR 2: 426 (Col. Waddell's Report — 20th GA)

The Wheatfield & Rose Woods

The Wheatfield at Gettysburg witnessed some of the bloodiest and most concentrated fighting during the battle. For over two and a half hours, more than 60 infantry units were engaged in and around this 20-acre field. Left behind were more than 4,000 dead and wounded soldiers from both armies. Union and Confederate control of the

Wheatfield changed rapidly five times, more than any other portion of the battlefield. Attacks and counterattacks came from all directions creating such a "vortex" that early veterans, guides, and tourbooks referred to the fighting here as a "whirl-pool" of battle.

At first, only Colonel Regis DeTrobriand's Brigade and Captain George Winslow's Battery guarded this area between Devil's Den and the Peach Orchard. When Confederates struck Devil's Den, DeTrobriand moved his brigade to the southwest corner of the Wheatfield with his left, held by the 17th Maine, along a stone wall. His right extended along a branch of Plum Run in the Rose Woods. DeTrobriand could hear fighting, but his visibility was limited. The south and west sides of the field were bordered by the Rose Woods. The western side also had a bouldered knoll that officers called the "stony hill." On the north side of the wheatfield was a road (today called the Wheatfield Road) and the Trostle Woods. On its east side ran a stone wall and a wood lot along Houck's Ridge.

Around 5 p.m., Brigadier General George "Tige" Anderson's Confederate brigade advanced through the Rose Woods and struck DeTrobriand's line. DeTrobriand's men turned them back. At some point, two Union brigades under Colonels Joseph Sweitzer and William Tilton got into position on the stony hill to reinforce DeTrobriand's right. The fighting lasted for about an hour when Brigadier General Joseph Kershaw's Confederate brigade reached the Rose farm to extend Anderson's left. Together, the two brigades made a second assault. Anderson was severely wounded, but his men pushed through the Rose Woods while Kershaw struck the stony hill and Peach Orchard. Tilton and Sweitzer's brigades retired from the stony hill, leaving DeTrobriand alone and well outnumbered. Once Kershaw's troops occupied the stony hill woods, they directed their fire on Winslow's battery out in the middle of the field. Winslow was forced to withdraw his guns. DeTrobriand feared his men would be surrounded and ordered them to fall back. After the 17th Maine fell back to the Wheatfield Road, they made a daring countercharge back into the Wheatfield where they fought to buy time until reinforcements came.

Just arrived in the Trostle Woods were four brigades of Brigadier General John Caldwell's Division. Some of Anderson's Confederates were already in the Wheatfield when Caldwell sent Colonel Edward Cross' Brigade against them. The brigade charged and "drove the enemy back to the far end of the wheatfield," but soon Colonel Cross was mortally wounded in the east edge of the Rose Woods. Meanwhile, within minutes of Cross' charge, Caldwell had sent Brigadier

General Samuel Zook's Brigade and Colonel Patrick Kelly's "Irish" Brigade to charge against the stony hill area. Zook was mortally wounded while leading the attack, but the two brigades were able to retake the stony hill, capturing a number of prisoners and forcing Kershaw to withdraw back to the Rose farmhouse. The last of Caldwell's brigades was Colonel John Brooke's, which Caldwell sent to relieve Cross' troops who had run out of ammunition. Halfway across the Wheatfield, Brooke ordered his men to fix bayonets and they charged into the south Rose Woods and drove Anderson's Georgians completely out. The Wheatfield and all the woods around it were again in Federal hands, but only for about 20 minutes. Anderson's Confederates at the Rose Farm were reinforced by Brigadier General Paul Semmes' Brigade, and Kershaw noticed Brigadier General William Wofford's Brigade "coming in in splendid style" from the Peach Orchard down the Wheatfield road. The Confederates now launched a third assault, and "completely outflanked" Caldwell's right on the stony hill, which gave way. Soon the remainder of Caldwell's Division was in full retreat. "In passing back over the wheatfield, I found the enemy had nearly closed in my rear," wrote Colonel Brooke.

Caldwell had called on Sweitzer's Brigade and Brigadier General Romeyn Ayres' U.S. Regulars for support. Minutes before Caldwell's men retreated, Sweitzer charged south across the Wheatfield to support them. But upon reaching the south stone wall, Sweitzer's regiments were suddenly fired upon from the rear. Kershaw's and Wofford's Confederates were rushing through the woods on stony hill. "I'll be ____ if I don't think we are faced the wrong way!" exclaimed Sweitzer's color bearer. Sweitzer immediately directed the 62nd New York and the 4th Michigan to face about and stop them, which they did and the two regiments became "mixed up with the enemy, and many hand-to-hand conflicts occurred." In the melee, "Colonel Jeffords, commanding the Fourth Michigan, was thrust through with a bayonet while gallantly attempting to rescue his colors from the grasp of the enemy." Surrounded, Sweitzer's Brigade fled. At about this time, Ayres' Regulars, who had been waiting at the east stone wall, wheeled left into the Wheatfield. They were immediately struck on their right and rear by the Confederates coming down the Wheatfield road and had to retreat, suffering enormous losses.

The combined onslaught by Anderson, Semmes, Kershaw, and Wofford routed the Federals out of the Wheatfield, across Plum Run valley, all the way to the northern base of Little Round Top. There, Brigadier General Samuel Crawford's Pennsylvania Reserves, Captain Frank Gibbs'

Battery and Colonel David Nevin's Brigade waited for them. Gibbs' Battery had just unlimbered, and Nevin's infantry had only recently arrived (the head of General John Sedgwick's 6th Corps) after marching "nearly 34 miles" that day. As Crawford saw it, "The plain to my front was covered with [Yankee] fugitives from all divisions, who rushed through my lines and along the road to my rear." Coming behind them was an "irregular, yelling line of the enemy." When Confederates reached the base of Little Round Top, Crawford ordered his Reserves to fire and charge, which they did "driving the enemy back." In the charge, Crawford grabbed a flag and led his men across the Plum Run valley to the stone wall at the eastern edge of the Wheatfield. Gibbs' Battery and Nevin's Brigade opened fire as well. Nevin's troops joined on Crawford's right in pursuit across the Weikert Farm as Wofford's Confederates retired. Crawford's men had "a desperate struggle" at the east stone wall, but they gained it and forced the Confederates to fall back across the Wheatfield. There behind the stone wall, Crawford's men settled in as darkness came, while across their front Confederates occupied the Rose Woods. The Wheatfield remained a no-man's land, too dangerous for the wounded laying there to receive help that night.

DESCRIPTION OF
    OR 1: 386 (Col. Kelly's Brigade Report)
    OR 1: 389 (Lieut. Smith's Report — 69th NY)
    OR 1: 653 (Gen. Crawford's Division Report)
    OR 2: 367 (Gen. Kershaw's Brigade Report)

THE CONFEDERATES STRIKE DETROBRIAND'S BRIGADE TWICE
    OR 1: 483, 484-485 (Gen. Birney's Division Report) — Colonel DeTrobriand's "gallant holding [of] his advanced position" during the fight earns him a promotion recommendation from Birney to the rank of Brigadier General.
    OR 1: 520-521 (Col. DeTrobriand's Brigade Report)
    OR 1: 522-523 (Col. Merrill's Report** — 17th ME) — The 17th Maine twice advances across the Wheatfield.
    OR 1: 525 (Col. Pulford's Report — 5th MI)
    OR 1: 528 (Maj. Rogers' Report — 110th PA) — Fought for two hours before retiring from the field.
    OR 1: 587 (Capt. Winslow's Battery Report) — Sees Smith's Battery retire from Devil's Den.
    OR 1: 601-602 & 604 (Gen. Barnes' Division Report**)
    OR 1: 607-608 (Col. Tilton's Brigade Report)
    OR 1: 610-612 (Col. Sweitzer's Brigade Report**)
    OR 2: 368 (Gen. Kershaw's Brigade Report**) — Kershaw's right occupies Stony Hill.

OR 2: 372 (Maj. Maffett's Report — 3rd SC) — Occupies Stony Hill.
OR 2: 397 (Col. White's Report — Anderson's Brigade)
OR 2: 399 (Capt. Hillyer's Report — 9th GA)
OR 2: 401 (Maj. McDaniel's Report — 11th GA)

CALDWELL'S DIVISION FIGHTS 'EM BACK
OR 1: 379-380 (Gen. Caldwell's Division Report)
OR 1: 381-382 (Col. McKeen's Report — Cross' Brigade) — Col. Cross is killed.
OR 1: 386 (Col. Kelly's Brigade Report)
OR 1: 389 (Lieut. Smith's Report — 69th NY)
OR 1: 390 (Capt. Burke's Report — 88th NY) — Wm. McClelland's bravery.
OR 1: 392 (Maj. Mulholland's Report** — 116th PA) — Fighting on Stony Hill.
OR 1: 394-395 (Col. Fraser's Report — Zook's Brigade) — Gen. Zook is killed.
OR 1: 395-396 (Capt. Scherrer's Report — 52nd NY)
OR 1: 396-397 (Col. Chapman's Report — 57th NY)
OR 1: 398 (Maj. Nelson's Report** — 66th NY)
OR 1: 400-401 (Col. Brooke's Brigade Report) — Colonel Merwin is killed.
OR 1: 403 (Col. Baily's Report — 2nd DE)
OR 1: 407 (Maj. Bradley's Report — 64th NY)
OR 1: 409-412 (Col. McMichael's Reports — 53rd PA) — Brooke's bayonet charge.
OR 1: 414 (Capt. Reynolds' Report — 145th PA)
OR 1: 415 (Capt. Oliver's Report — 145th PA)
OR 1: 483 (Gen. Birney's Division Report)
OR 2: 368 (Gen. Kershaw's Brigade Report**)
OR 2: 372 (Maj. Maffett's Report** — 3rd SC)
OR 2: 397 (Col. White's Report — Anderson's Brigade)
OR 2: 399 (Capt. Hillyer's Report — 9th GA)
OR 2: 401 (Maj. McDaniel's Report — 11th GA)
OR 2: 403 (Maj. Gee's Report — 59th GA)
OR 2: 409 (Col. Work's Report — 1st TX)
OR 2: 422 (Col. DuBose's Report — 15th GA)

SWEITZER'S BRIGADE FIGHTS HAND-TO-HAND
OR 1: 601-602 & 604 (Gen. Barnes' Division Report**)
OR 1: 610-612 (Col. Sweitzer's Brigade Report**) — Colonel Jeffords "was thrust through with a bayonet in a contest over his colors …"
OR 2: 369 (Gen. Kershaw's Brigade Report) — Kershaw claims the "fighting was general and desperate" and feared his men would be surrounded.

AYRES ON THE SCENE
OR 1: 593 (Gen. Sykes' V Corps Report)
OR 1: 634-635 (Gen. Ayres' Division Report)

OR 1: 639 (Capt. Adams' Report — 4th U.S.) — Claims the fighting ended about 7:00 p.m.
OR 1: 640-641 (Capt. Dunn's Report — 12th U.S.)
OR 1: 643 (Major Giddings' Report — 14th U.S.)
OR 1: 644-645 (Col. Burbank's Brigade Report) — Claims they withdrew with it was "nearly dark."
OR 1: 646-647 (Maj. Lee's Report** — 2nd U.S.)
OR 1: 647-648 (Capt. Hancock's Report — 7th U.S.)
OR 1: 648-649 (Capt. Clinton's Report — 10th U.S.)
OR 1: 649-650 (Maj. Floyd-Jones' Report** -- 11th U.S.)
OR 1: 650-651 (Col. Greene's Report — 17th U.S.)

CONFEDERATES ROUT THE YANKS TO LITTLE ROUND TOP
OR 2: 369 (Gen. Kershaw's Brigade Report**)
OR 2: 397 (Col. White's Report — Anderson's Brigade) — "The third advance ... resulted ... in the rout of the enemy".
OR 2: 399-400 (Capt. Hillyer's Report — 9th GA)
OR 2: 401-402 (Maj. McDaniel's Report — 11th GA)
OR 2: 403 (Maj. Gee's Report — 59th GA)
OR 2: 422 (Col. Dubose's Report — 15th GA)

CRAWFORD'S CHARGE REPELS THE REBELS
OR 1: 593 (Gen. Sykes' V Corps Report)
OR 1: 652-654, 655 (Gen. Crawford's Division Report**)
OR 1: 657 (McCandless' Brigade Report)
OR 1: 660 (Capt. Martin's Artillery Report) — Walcott's Massachusetts battery was captured by Wofford's Confederates and recaptured by Nevin's brigade.
OR 1: 662 (Capt. Gibbs' Battery Report**)
OR 1: 684-685 (Col. Nevin's Report** — Wheaton's Brigade) — The 62nd NY, 93rd PA, 98th PA, and 139th PA supported Crawford's charge.
OR 1: 688 (Col. Moody's Report** — 139th PA) — Marched "all night" and day 36 miles to reach Gettysburg by 3 p.m. and then joined the charge.

LOSSES FROM WHEATFIELD ENGAGEMENT
OR 1: 407 (Col. Bradley's Report — 64th NY) — See table.
OR 1: 412 (Col. McMichael's Reports — 53rd PA) — Lost 70 per cent!
OR 1: 613 (Col. Sweitzer's Brigade Report) — Lost nearly half of his brigade!

The Peach Orchard & Rose Farm

The fight at the Peach Orchard, like that in the Wheatfield, involved the engagement of over 60 units from the two armies. But in this instance, over half were batteries. More than 50 Federal guns supported Union Major General Daniel Sickles' advanced line here. Other than Cemetery Hill, this area was the next most-concentrated place of Union artillery on July 2. The Confederates had nearly the same number of guns along Warfield and Seminary ridges aimed to converge their fire on the orchard from the south and west.

When Sickles advanced his Corps, his two divisions formed a salient at the Sherfy peach orchard. Here, his troops were closer to their enemy on Seminary Ridge than they were to their own army on Cemetery Ridge. Sickles' left division under Major General David Birney was stretched the farthest. "My line," wrote Birney, "was formed with Ward on the left [at the Den], DeTrobriand in the center [in the Wheatfield], and Graham on my right at the Peach Orchard." Brigadier General Charles Graham's Brigade fronted the Emmitsburg Road with the Sherfy farmhouse and barn in their front, which some of his men occupied. But with his brigade facing west, a considerable gap was created to their left between them and DeTrobriand's Brigade in the Wheatfield. To fill this gap, Brigadier General Henry Hunt, the Chief of Artillery, helped to place several batteries into position along the Wheatfield Road. Most of these batteries belonged to Lieutenant Colonel Freeman McGilvery's Reserve Artillery Brigade. Now 30 guns were facing south toward the Rose Farm but they had few infantry regiments in support. Sickles' right division, commanded by Brigadier General Andrew Humphreys, faced west and continued the line formed by Graham's Brigade. This line of infantry ran along the Emmitsburg Road almost reaching the Codori farm.

Around 4:00 p.m., Longstreet's Confederate batteries opened on the advanced Federal position. An hour-long artillery duel ensued. "The fire from our lines and from the enemy became [so] incessant," remembered one Confederate artillery officer, "[that we] sometimes [had] to pause and allow the smoke to clear away, in order to enable the gunners to take aim." The salient created by Sickles' at the peach orchard exposed both his south-facing and west-facing units to frontal and enfilade fire from the Rebel guns. Sickles' infantry was ordered to lay down to minimize casualties, but several units suffered heavy losses from this crossfire. "Owing to the peculiar formation of the line," remembered one Union officer, "we were at times exposed to a heavy cross-fire." The "enfilade fire...was inflicting serious damage through the whole line of my command," wrote Colonel McGilvery.

Sometime after 5:00 p.m., Confederate Brigadier General Joseph Kershaw advanced his brigade of South Carolinians across McGilvery's front toward the Rose Farm. The Federal gunners fired into the exposed flank of the southerners. Kershaw ordered the regiments on the left of his line to swing north and attack the artillery. McGilvery's batteries repulsed two attacks and forced Kershaw's troops "to shelter themselves in masses around the [Rose] house and barn." There the Confederates had little protection from Federal artillery fire. As McGilvery recalled, "After the battle, I visited...the house and barn...and found 120 odd dead, belonging to three South Carolina regiments."

Suddenly, around 6:00 p.m., Confederate Bridagier General William Barksdale's four Mississippi regiments joined the assault on the Peach Orchard. According to witnesses, Barksdale's men charged in three lines, yelling as they came, and struck with remarkable speed, taking numerous prisoners at the Sherfy house and barn. The "enemy...advanced so quickly and in such force," observed Union Captain Edward Bowen, that his 114th Pennsylvania regiment was so completely scattered that he was still looking for his troops into the night. Barksdale's men outnumbered Graham's troops and within a half-hour of the attack Graham's men started giving up ground. The Sherfy barn was in flames by this time and Captain Bowen later reported "a number of [my] men [are] missing whom I have no doubt were killed and their bodies burned when the barn was burned down." Soon Generals Graham and Sickles were casualties too. Graham had been wounded and captured in the orchard, while Sickles, who had been watching the attack from near the Trostle barn, was struck in the right leg by a 12-pounder solid shot. Sickles transferred command to General Birney and was carried off the field to a hospital where his leg was amputated.

Soon McGilvery's batteries were nearly surrounded. Kershaw's South Carolineans had gained the Stony Hill on the gunners' left, and Barksdale's Mississippians were closing in on their right. Graham's line crumbled. Exposed to "fire from both flanks and front," they withdrew and several units narrowly escaped total destruction. Two batteries, Bigelow's and Phillips', retired "by prolonge." This was a dangerous and difficult maneuver where, with each shot at the enemy, the gun was withdrawn a short distance using the recoil to help move the cannon off the field. And it cost them their horses severely. "Captain Phillips [and 5] men hauled one of his pieces off by hand [because] every horse in the limbers [had] been shot down." Bigelow's battery was the last to withdraw, and as the batteries pulled back toward the Trostle house, McGilvery "gave Captain Bigelow orders to hold his position...at all hazards" to cover the retreat. Backed into the corner of two stone walls across from the Trostle farmhouse, Bigelow arranged his six cannon in a semi-circle and fought off the Confederates coming from the west and south until the enemy entered his battery. Bigelow was shot but got out alive with the help of his bugler.

However, "more than half of his men," 60 horses, and four of his guns were lost.

Meanwhile, Sickles' right division under Humphreys was the last to retreat. At Birney's order, Humphreys threw back his left. New Yorkers of the "Excelsior" brigade held the left flank. They were immediately struck by Barksdale who had turned three of his regiments north from the Peach Orchard to roll up the Union line. Within minutes, Wilcox and Lang's Confederate brigades also struck Humphreys' front. In addition, Confederate guns quickly moved up to the Peach Orchard where they could enfilade Humphreys' line. Outnumbered and subjected to a crossfire, one Union officer described how his "men were falling on every side" and that only "a few minutes could elapse before the entire line would be shot down." The officer ranks of the 11th New Jersey were so decimated that command passed down to the adjutant. Birney ordered Humphreys to retreat, and, in so doing, the division suffered its greatest losses. Several Union officers claimed their regiments withdrew "slowly," "stubbornly," and "in good order," but from the Confederates' perspective, the last of Sickles' line simply "broke and fled in confusion."

ARTILLERY DUEL

- OR 1: 483 (Gen. Birney's Division Report) — Confederate artillery enfiladed Graham's Brigade.
- OR 1: 500 (Col. Craig's Report — 105th PA)
- OR 1: 504 (Col. Madill's Report — 141st PA) — These Yanks "sustained a considerable loss" from the artillery barrage.
- OR 1: 507-508 (Col. Lakeman's Report — 3rd ME)
- OR 1: 559 (Col. Brewster's Brigade Report) — The Excelsior Brigade suffered many casualties from "the enemy's artillery."
- OR 1: 566 (Col. Austin's Report — 72nd NY)
- OR 1: 568 (Capt. Lockwood's Report — 120th NY)
- OR 1: 581-583 (Capt. Randolph's Artillery Report**)
- OR 1: 570 (Col. Burling's Brigade Report)
- OR 1: 575 (Capt. Woolsey's Report — 5th NJ)
- OR 1: 585-586 (Capt. Clark's Battery Report)
- OR 1: 587 (Capt. Winslow's Battery Report) — Winslow's Battery fired from the Wheatfield.
- OR 1: 589-590 (Lieut. Freeborn's Report — Bucklyn's Battery)
- OR 1: 590-591 (Lieut. James' Report — Seeley's Battery)
- OR 1: 881 (Col. McGilvery's Artillery Report)
- OR 1: 885 (Capt. Phillips' Battery Report)
- OR 1: 886 (Lieut. Milton's Report — Bigelow's Battery)

OR 1: 887 (Capt. Hart's Battery Report**)
OR 1: 889-890 (Capt. Thompson's Battery Report)
OR 1: 900-901 (Capt. Ames' Battery Report**)
OR 2: 375 (Col. Cabell's Battalion Report**)
OR 2: 379 (Capt. McCarthy's Battery Report)
OR 2: 380 (Capt. Manly's Battery Report)
OR 2: 382 (Lieut. Furlong's Report — Fraser's Battery)
OR 2: 384 (Lieut. Motes' Report — Carlton's Battery)
OR 2: 429 (Col. Alexander's Battalion Report)
OR 2: 432 (Capt. Taylor's Battery Report**) — Read about the deaths of gunners William Ray and Joseph Lantz.
OR 2: 617-618 (Gen. Wilcox's Brigade Report)

KERSHAW'S CONFEDERATES STRIKE ACROSS THE ROSE FARM
OR 1: 504-505 (Col. Madill's Report — 141st PA)
OR 1: 508 (Col. Lakeman's Report — 3rd ME) — These Yanks faced "four times their number" in the attack.
OR 1: 523-524 (Col. Pierce's Report** — 3rd MI) — Confederates made several attempts to take the Rose Farm, but were repulsed.
OR 1: 574 (Col. Bailey's Report** — 2nd NH)
OR 1: 583-584 (Capt. Randolph's Artillery Report)
OR 1: 585-586 (Capt. Clark's Battery Report)
OR 1: 881-882 (Col. McGilvery's Artillery Report**)
OR 1: 887 (Capt. Hart's Battery Report**)
OR 1: 889 (Lieut. McMahon's Report — Hart's Battery)
OR 1: 901 (Capt. Ames' Battery Report) — Ames' battery is relieved by Watson's battery "at 5:30 p.m.," before Barksdale's charge commences.
OR 2: 367-368 (Gen. Kershaw's Brigade Report**)

BARKSDALE'S CHARGE CLEARS THE PEACH ORCHARD
OR 1: 483-484 (Gen. Birney's Division Report) — The 141st PA lost 149 of 200 men "taken into the fight" (p. 484).
OR 1: 497 (Capt. Nelson's Report — 57th PA) — Barksdale advanced "in three lines."
OR 1: 499 (Col. Tippin's Report — 68th PA) — Gen. Graham "was severely wounded" and captured.
OR 1: 500-501 (Col. Craig's Report** — 105th PA)
OR 1: 502-3 (Capt. Bowen's Report — 114th PA)
OR 1: 505 (Col. Madill's Report — 141st PA) — Madill criticizes the early withdrawal of Humphreys' Division.
OR 1: 508 (Col. Lakeman's Report — 3rd ME) — These Yanks faced "four times their number."
OR 1: 524 (Col. Pierce's Report — 3rd MI)
OR 1: 574 (Col. Bailey's Report** — 2nd NH)

OR 1: 590 (Lieut. Freeborn's Report — Bucklyn's Battery)
OR 1: 583-584 (Capt. Randolph's Artillery Report)
OR 1: 586 (Capt. Clark's Battery Report)
OR 1: 872 (Gen. Tyler's Artillery Report)
OR 1: 887 (Capt. Hart's Battery Report)
OR 1: 889 (Lieut. McMahon's Report — Hart's Battery)
OR 1: 890 (Capt. Thompson's Battery Report**)

BIGELOW'S & PHILLIPS' BATTERIES RETIRE BY PROLONGE
OR 1: 875 (Gen. Tyler's Artillery Report) — Read about Lieutenant Milton
OR 1: 882 & 884 (Col. McGilvery's Artillery Report**)
OR 1: 885 (Capt. Phillips' Battery Report)
OR 1: 886 (Lieut. Milton's Report — Bigelow's Battery)

SICKLES LOSES HIS RIGHT LEG
OR 1: 483 (Gen. Birney's Division Report)
OR 1: 533 (Humphreys' Division Report)

THE SHERFY BARN BURNS
OR 1: 503 (Capt. Bowen's Report — 114th PA)

CONFEDERATE GUNS OCCUPY THE PEACH ORCHARD
OR 2: 430 (Col. E. P. Alexander's Artillery Report)
OR 2: 432 (Capt. Taylor's Battery Report)

SICKLES' RIGHT RETREATS LAST
OR 1: 483 (Gen. Birney's Division Report)
OR 1: 533 (Gen. Humphreys' Division Report)
OR 1: 543 (Gen. Carr's Brigade Report) — Carr indicates that the "Collis Zouaves" [114th Pennsylvania] "gave way" first.
OR 1: 549 (Col. Tripp's Report — 11th MA)
OR 1: 551 (Capt. Donovan's Report — 16th MA)
OR 1: 553 (Col. McAllister's Report** — 11th NJ)
OR 1: 553-555 (Lieut. John Schoonover** — 11th NJ) — Command of the 11th New Jersey passed four times due to the severity of the fight!
OR 1: 559 (Col. Brewster's Report** — Excelsior Brigade)
OR 1: 563 (Maj. Hugo's Report — 70th NY) — Suffered 112 casualties.
OR 1: 565 (Col. Potter's Report — 71st NY) — Lost 7 of 13 officers.
OR 1: 566 (Col. Austin's Report — 72nd NY)
OR 1: 568-569 (Capt. Lockwood's Report — 120th NY) — Suffered 203 casualties. Color bearer, Corporal William O'Brien, receives exceptional praise.
OR 1: 575-576 (Capt. Woolsey's Report** — 5th NJ)
OR 1: 576-577 (Col. Sewell's Report — 5th NJ)
OR 1: 591 (Lieut. James' Report** — Seeley's Battery) — Several captured cannoneers "succeeded in making their escape and returned to the battery."

OR 2: 614 (Gen. Anderson's Division Report)
OR 2: 618 (Gen. Wilcox's Brigade Report**) — Wilcox describes the terrain and what it was like to cross the obstacles of stone and plank fences.
OR 2: 631 (Col. Lang's Report — Perry's Brigade)

The Codori-Trostle Thicket & Cemetery Ridge

The Confederate rout of Sickles' 3rd Corps from the Peach Orchard opened a huge gap in the Federal line and Union Major General Winfield Scott Hancock had to fill it. He could see the enemy "pressing vigorously" toward South Cemetery Ridge where, in the words of another officer, "an interval of nearly a quarter of a mile was opened." It was nearly dusk as Barksdale, Wilcox, and Lang's brigades pursued the retreating Yankees to a thicket along Plum Run that traversed the Codori and Trostle farms. After losing Bigelow's four guns at the Trostle farm, Union Colonel Freeman McGilvery made an admirable stand at Plum Run to delay the Confederates with the remnants of his artillery brigade and two reinforcing batteries, but there he lost several more guns to Barksdale's advancing troops.

Along Plum Run the Confederates regrouped; there seemed to be no one left in their way, but not for long. General Hancock had ridden down Cemetery Ridge leading Colonel George Willard's New York brigade to the gap and ordered them into action. They charged Barksdale's Mississippians with the bayonet, forcing them to withdraw, and recaptured some of McGilvery's guns. Willard's men pushed all the way to the Peach Orchard where they were turned back by Confederate artillery. As their engagement came to a close, both units had lost their commanders. Willard was killed by a shell as he returned across Plum Run, and Barksdale lay mortally wounded on the field.

The main threat to the Federal gap came from Major General Richard Anderson's Division of A. P. Hill's Corps. Four of Anderson's brigades — Wilcox's, Lang's, Wright's, and Posey's — were advancing progressively toward Cemetery Ridge. Wilcox's Brigade of Alabamans was in the lead and had advanced dangerously close to the Union line under the cover of Plum Run's thicket. As General Hancock rode back up the Federal line, their shots hit Hancock's aide twice. According to Wilcox, Cemetery Ridge was "almost won," but then a "line of infantry descended the slope in front at a double-quick." It was troops of the 1st Minnesota regiment. Fortunately, Hancock had found them at the last minute and ordered them to attack, which they did bravely with their bayonets.

No troops received higher praise that day from Hancock than those of the 1st Minnesota. As he stated in his report, "I cannot speak too highly of this regiment and its commander in its attack ... [in] which it lost three-fourths of the officers and men engaged." The regiment was not even at full strength, being only eight companies present with three detached elsewhere. As Wilcox remembered, "Three several times did this last of the enemy's lines attempt to drive my men back, and were as often repulsed." In short, the Minnesotans were annihilated. A total of 262 made their charge to Plum Run, and only 47 came back (a loss of 82 percent of those engaged). They were outnumbered more than three-to-one, but they stalled Wilcox's Brigade for about 15 minutes until enough Federal reinforcements arrived. Eventually Wilcox withdrew after taking fire from some of Willard's troops on his right, from rallied remnants of Sickles' Corps on his front, from artillery fire on both front and flank, and having received no reinforcements from his commander, General Anderson. Coming up on Wilcox's left was Lang's Brigade of Floridians. They had advanced nearly as far when Colonel Lang learned "that General Wilcox had fallen back." Federal troops were rallying in strength, and out of fear of being isolated and surrounded, Lang ordered his brigade to retreat as well.

From where the Virginia State Memorial stands today, Brigadier General Ambrose Wright advanced his brigade of Georgians for Cemetery Ridge. It was about 6:00 p.m. when he ordered his men forward in concert with Wilcox's and Lang's Brigades. Immediately to his north, Posey's Brigade of Mississippians followed. But Posey's men had the William Bliss house and barn in their front, situated midway between the lines, and there they were stalled by the 1st Delaware and 12th New Jersey regiments. The Bliss farm had already been a scene of much skirmishing that afternoon, having exchanged hands twice, and Union and Confederate prisoners were both captured there. Posey's Confederates eventually took the Bliss barn and house for good that evening, but most of the brigade never advanced beyond the Emmitsburg Road.

Wright's Brigade was the only Confederate unit to pierce the Federal line on Cemetery Ridge that evening. His Georgians, numbering about 1000, stormed over the Emmitsburg Road and came around both sides of the Codori barn, forcing back several Union regiments and batteries, and capturing numerous prisoners and several guns. A gap still existed south of the Copse of Trees. It was a hole in Brigadier General John Gibbon's Division that Gibbon later explained was "opened by detaching troops to other points." When the left of Wright's Brigade seized several more guns within 30 yards of Gibbon's line at the Copse, and planted a "battle-flag upon one of them," the Federals opened fire, pouring a dozen bullets into the rebel color-bearer alone. Gibbon's men fought furiously and prevented the Georgians from breaching their position at the Copse, but the rest of Wright's Brigade seemed unstoppable. "The enemy," wrote Gibbon, "came on with such impetuosity that the head of his column came quite through [the] vacancy in our line to the left[.]" The right of Wright's Brigade, amounting to about 500 men, had charged into the gap and seized the center of Cemetery Ridge momentarily. "We were now complete masters of the field," wrote General Wright, "having gained the key...of the enemy's whole line."

But it was impossible for Wright's men to stay in their position and to further exploit their success. They had fought for "an hour or more," they never received reinforcements, and they had no protection on their left and right flanks. It was sunset, and they were alone and in danger of being surrounded as darkness set in. "We were now in a critical condition," wrote Wright. "The enemy [was rapidly converging upon us]...and with painful hearts we abandoned our captured guns, faced about, and prepared to cut our way through the closing lines in our rear." As Federal forces counterattacked them, two regiments stood out: The 13th Vermont chased them head-on with the bayonet and captured dozens at the Emmitsburg Road, and the 106th Pennsylvania made a bayonet charge from the right and captured about 250 at the Codori farm. Wright claimed his brigade had seized 20 Union cannon in their assault, but all were recovered by the Federals in the repulse. Wright's Brigade suffered 688 casualties. They had penetrated further than Pickett would, against most of the very troops who would fight back Pickett's Division the next day. There is no better example of their fortitude than the 48th Georgia, whose colors "were shot down no less than seven times" before finally being lost.

In a dispatch to Washington the next morning, Meade avoided any mention of this close call, except for one outcome: "General Barksdale's...dead body is within our lines."

DESCRIPTION OF
    OR 1: 476 (Capt. Seeley's Report — 111th NY)
    OR 2: 618 (Gen. Wilcox's Brigade Report**)

MCGILVERY'S GUNS AT PLUM RUN
    OR 1: 660 (Capt. Martin's Artillery Report**) — Watson's battery is abandoned.
    OR 1: 872 (Gen. Tyler's Artillery Report)
    OR 1: 882-883 (Col. McGilvery's Artillery Report)
    OR 1: 890 (Capt. Thompson's Battery Report)

OR 1: 897-898 (Lieut. Dow's Battery Report**)

WILLARD'S BRIGADE CHARGE

OR 1: 370-371 (Gen. Hancock's II Corps Report) — Hancock ordered Willard to charge.
OR 1: 472 (Col. Bull's Report** — Willard's Brigade) — Willard's death.
OR 1: 474-475 (Col. MacDougall's Report — 111th NY)
OR 1: 475-476 (Capt. Seeley's Report — 111th NY) — Recovery of Watson's guns.
OR 1: 477 (Lieut. Haskell — 125th NY)

BARKSDALE'S DEATH

OR 1: 74 (Gen. Meade's Dispatch) — "General Barksdale's...dead body is within our lines."
OR 1: 371 (Gen. Hancock's II Corps Report)
OR 1: 436 (Col. Hall's Brigade Report)
OR 2: 359 (Gen. Longstreet's I Corps Report)

THE CHARGE OF THE 1ST MINNESOTA

OR 1: 371 (Gen. Hancock's Report) — Hancock ordered the 1st Minn. to charge.
OR 1: 419 & 420 (Gen. Harrow's Division Report)
OR 1: 425 (Capt. Coates' Report — 1st MN)

FEDERALS RALLY AGAINST WILCOX AND LANG'S BRIGADES

OR 1: 416-417 (Gen. Gibbon's Division Report)
OR 1: 442-443 (Col. Devereux's Report** — 19th MA)
OR 1: 451 (Col. Mallon's Report — 42nd NY)
OR 1: 533 (Gen. Humphreys' Division Report)
OR 1: 543 (Gen. Carr's Brigade Report)
OR 1: 551 (Capt. Donovan's Report — 16th MA)
OR 1: 554 (Lieut. John Schoonover — 11th NJ)
OR 1: 559 (Col. Brewster's Brigade Report) — The rallied troops of the Excelsior Brigade captured the colors of the 8th Florida.
OR 1: 565 (Col. Potter's Report — 71st NY)
OR 1: 566 (Col. Austin's Report — 72nd NY)
OR 1: 568 (Capt. Lockwood's Report — 120th NY) — Use of bayonet.
OR 2: 608 (Gen. Hill's III Corps Report)
OR 2: 614 (Gen. Anderson's Division Report)
OR 2: 618-619, 620 (Gen. Wilcox's Brigade Report**) — read of Col. Forney
OR 2: 631-632 (Col. Lang's Brigade Report**)

THE BLISS FARM FIGHT

OR 1: 453 (Gen. Hays' Division Report)
OR 1: 464-465 (Col. Smyth's Brigade Report)
OR 1: 469 (Lieut. Dent's Report — 1st DE) — Hancock's arrest of Col. Harris.
OR 1: 470 (Maj. Hill's Report — 12th NJ)

OR 2: 633-634 (Gen. Posey's Brigade Report)
OR 2: 634-635 (Col. Harris' Report — 19th MS)

Wright's Brigade Pierces The Union Center
OR 1: 417 (Gen. Gibbon's Division Report)
OR 1: 419-420 (Gen. Harrow's Division Report)
OR 1: 423 (Col. Joslin's Report — 15th MA)
OR 1: 426 (Capt. Darrow's Report — 82nd NY) — Captures the 48th Ga. colors.
OR 1: 427 (Gen. Webb's Brigade Report)
OR 1: 431 (Capt. Davis' Report — 69th PA)
OR 1: 432 (Col. Smith's Report — 71st PA)
OR 1: 436-437 (Col. Hall's Brigade Report) — Confederates get within 30 yards of Hall's brigade.
OR 1: 445 (Capt. Abbot's Report — 20th Mass)
OR 1: 447-448 (Maj. Curtis' Report** — 7th Mich)
OR 1: 452 (Capt. McFadden's Report — 59th NY)
OR 1: 478 (Capt. Hazard's Artillery Report) — Brown's Battery lost 30 horses.
OR 1: 880 Lieut. Weir's Battery Report) — Lost three guns.
OR 2: 608 (Gen. Hill's III Corps Report)
OR 2: 614 (Gen. Anderson's Division Report)
OR 2: 623-625 (Gen. Wright's Brigade Report**)
OR 2: 627-628 (Col. Walker's Report** — 3rd GA) — Claims they seized 11 Federal guns!
OR 2: 628-629 (Capt. McCurry's Report — 22nd GA)
OR 2: 629 (Capt. Hall's Report — 48th GA)
OR 2: 630 (Capt. Moffett's Report** — 2nd GA Battalion)

Countercharges Of The 13th Vermont And The 106th Pennsylvania
OR 1: 258 (Gen. Doubleday's Division Report)
OR 1: 349 (Gen. Stannard's Brigade Report)
OR 1: 351-352 (Col. Randall's Report** — 13th VT) — Recovered Weir's guns.
OR 1: 427 (Gen. Webb's Brigade Report) — Webb claims the 72nd Pennsylvania aided the 106th Pennsylvania in capturing prisoners, but the 72nd claimed they were never engaged.
OR 1: 434 (Col. Curry's Report** — 106th PA) — Captured 250 prisoners.

Gathering The Guns And The Wounded Left On The Field
OR 1: 422 (Gen. Harrow's Division Report) — Harrow's brigade collected 1,740 rifles and guns.
OR 1: 897-898 (Lieut. Dow's Battery Report**)
OR 1: 774 (Gen. Williams' XII Corps Report)
OR 1: 804 (Gen. Lockwood's Brigade Report)
OR 1: 805-806 (Col. Mausby's Report — 1st MD Potomac)
OR 1: 809 (Col. Ketcham's Report — 150th NY)

East Cemetery Hill

Around 4:00 p.m., shortly after Longstreet's guns opened the assault on the Federal left, Confederate Major Joseph Latimer's Battalion on Benner's Hill opened fire against Cemetery Hill, commencing a full-scale cannonade with Federal guns there. Latimer's Battalion belonged to Ewell's Corps and their action were part of a diversion called for by Lee's plan that day. Lee had ordered Longstreet's assault to be the "principal attack" and Ewell "to make a simultaneous demonstration upon the enemy's right, to be converted into a real attack should the opportunity offer." General Ewell subsequently ordered all three of his divisions to make an attack — Johnson's Division was to assault Culp's Hill, Early's Division was to strike Cemetery Hill from the east, and Rodes' Division was to strike Cemetery Hill from the northwest in coordination with Early.

Cemetery Hill held the main concentration of Union artillery with over 60 guns arranged in nearly all directions. On Seminary Ridge, additional Confederate guns from Ewell's Corps and some from Hill's Corps joined the bombardment which lasted about two hours. In concert with Latimer's guns, the shelling created a "most hellish cross-fire" for the Union troops and batteries on Cemetery Hill. But the Federal batteries fought back well. Half-way through the artillery duel, they had pounded Latimer's men and guns so thoroughly that Latimer had to withdraw "all but one battery, which he kept to repel any infantry advance." Major Latimer was only 19 years old but had already gained a reputation for bravery. Latimer remained with his last four guns as the cannonade came to a close. One of the last Federal shells exploded nearby and mortally wounded him in the arm. "No greater loss could have befallen the artillery of this corps," wrote General Ewell, "...his soldierly qualities had impressed me as deeply as those of any officer in my command." In surveying the *Official Records*, it appears no other Confederate officer's death was lamented in more reports than that of Major Latimer.

Around 7:00 p.m., Johnson's Division began their assault against Culp's Hill, and sometime thereafter General Early sent forward Hays' and Hokes' Brigades to attack Cemetery Hill. It "was a little before dusk," wrote Early of when he ordered his brigades to advance, while Brigadier General Harry Hays recalled receiving such orders "a little before 8 p.m." Attacking Cemetery Hill from the north and east would prove a difficult assault for its steepness and approach. According to one Confederate officer's report, the brigades had to traverse open terrain for "fully half a mile from our lines" just to get there.

Hays' Brigade of "Louisiana Tigers" charged across the open fields under heavy grape and canister fire, and fought their way up the northeast side of Cemetery Hill, breaking through "at least two [Union] lines of infantry posted behind stone and plank fences." Hays reported his men overcame a third line, driving out Union soldiers from rifle pits behind fallen timber half-way up the hill's slope. Union Major General Oliver Howard, whose 11th Corps troops faced the Tigers' onslaught, observed "the attack was so sudden and violent that the infantry in front of [Brigadier General Adelbert] Ames was giving way [and] at one moment the enemy had got within the batteries." Darkness and smoke, Hays claimed, aided their success because it prevented Union gunners from accurately shelling his men, which surely would have decimated them "in the full light of day." The Federal batteries breached were Wiedrich's and Ricketts', the former being completely overrun and the latter having one of its guns spiked by the enemy. Combat among the guns became desperate as Union cannoneers fought the Confederates "hand to hand with handspikes, rammers, and pistols...fence-rails and stones [.]" Hays claimed his men ultimately captured several of the guns and four stands of colors at the summit, after which "a quiet of several minutes" passed until "heavy masses" of Union reinforcements formed in his front and fired numerous volleys upon his brigade before forcing him to retire. This temporary capture and pause in the engagement at the summit is not how most of the Union reports describe the fighting, which instead suggest hand-to-hand fighting at the guns never ceased until the Confederates were driven off.

Meanwhile, Hoke's Brigade, under the command of Colonel Isaac Avery, struck at the depression between East Cemetery Hill and Steven's Knoll to its south. With his men climbing over a rail fence, they endured enfilading fire from both their left and right. Wheeling right, they charged against Union soldiers aligned behind three stone walls on the south side of the East Cemetery Hill. Attempting to join Hays men at the summit, they managed to penetrate all three walls as they escalated their way up, but the fire from behind and their tenuous position forced them to eventually retreat. In this amazing effort, Colonel Avery was shot in the throat, and as he lay mortally wounded in the darkness, he penciled on a piece of paper the following testament to his service: "I died with my face to the enemy."

It was competely dark when the fighting ended on East Cemetery Hill, and General Howard claimed it "lasted less than an hour." Major Samuel Tate of the 6th North Carolina of Hoke's Brigade vehemently complained to his state's governor that a lack of support prevented Confederate victory on Cemetery Hill. General Ewell attributed the problem to Rodes' Division, which failed to advance on Early's right. According to Major General Rodes, he had too much terrain to cover and was therefore late in getting into position. His men did commence an assault against Cemetery Hill from the northwest, "driving in the enemy's skirmishers," but it was dark and he learned Early's assault was already over. When his brigade commanders sent word that the ground and Union defenses of Cemetery Hill in their front appeared too formidable, he called off the attack.

The Cannonade & Death of Major Latimer

- OR 1: 363 (Lieut. Breck's Report — Reynolds' Battery)
- OR 1: 365 (Capt. Cooper's Battery Report) — Cooper's battery was relieved by Ricketts' arrival around 7 p.m., just prior to General Early's infantry attack.
- OR 1: 722 (Gen. Steinwehr's Division Report)
- OR 1: 730 (Gen. Schurz's Division Report)
- OR 1: 735 (Col. Dobke's Report — 45th NY)
- OR 1: 740 (Capt. Koenig's Report — 58th NY)
- OR 1: 749 (Maj. Osborn's Artillery Report)
- OR 1: 870 (Col. Muhlenberg's Report) — Knap's and Kinzie's batteries fire from Culp's Hill around 4:00 p.m.
- OR 1: 873 (Gen. Tyler's Artillery Report)
- OR 1: 891 (Capt. Taft's Battery Report)
- OR 1: 892 (Capt. Edgell's Battery Report)
- OR 1: 893-894 (Lieut. Norton's Battery Report)
- OR 1: 894 (Capt. Rickett's Battery Report)
- OR 2: 351 (Gen. Pendleton's Artillery Report) — The death of Major Latimer.
- OR 2: 446-447 (Gen. Ewell's II Corps Report**) — Death of Major Latimer. Ewell had Latimer open fire against Cemetery Hill upon hearing Longstreet's guns.
- OR 2: 456 (Col. Brown's Artillery Report) — Union guns on Cemetery Hill were "concentrated...so great." Confederate batteries fire from Seminary Ridge.
- OR 2: 504 & 505 (Gen. Johnson's Division Report) — Read about Major Latimer.
- OR 2: 531 (Gen. Jones' Brigade Report) — Latimer's Battalion moved into position around 4 p.m.
- OR 2: 543-544 (Col. Andrews' Report** — Latimer's Battalion) — These batteries fired from Benner's Hill. Read about Major Latimer.
- OR 2: 604 (Capt. Dance's Battalion Report) — His guns fired from near the Railroad Cut and the Seminary.
- OR 2: 610 (Col. Walker's Artillery Report)
- OR 2: 635 (Maj. Lane's Battalion Report)

OR 2: 652 (Col. Garnett's Battalion Report)
OR 2: 675 (Maj. McIntosh's Battalion Report)
OR 2: 679 (Capt. Brunson's Report — Pegram's Battalion)

Charge Of The Lousiana Tigers

OR 1: 358 (Col. Wainwright's Artillery Report)
OR 1: 361 (Lieut. Whittier's Report — Stevens' Battery)
OR 1: 363 (Lieut. Breck's Report — Reynolds' Battery)
OR 1: 705-706 (Gen. Howard's XI Corps Report**)
OR 1: 713 (Gen. Ames' Report — Barlow's Division)
OR 1: 714 (Col. von Einsiedel's Report — 41st NY)
OR 1: 715 (Col. Harris' Report — Ames' Brigade)
OR 1: 718 (Major Brady's Report — 17th CT)
OR 1: 722 (Gen. Steinwehr's Division Report)
OR 1: 752 (Capt. Wiedrich's Battery Report)
OR 2: 447 (Gen. Ewell's II Corps Report)
OR 2: 470-471 (Gen. Early's Division Report**)
OR 2: 480-482 (Gen. Hays' Brigade Report**)
OR 2: 484-485 (Col. Godwin's Report** — Hoke's Brigade)

Enfilading Fire From Steven's Knoll

OR 1: 361 (Lieut. Whittier's Report — Stevens' Battery)
OR 2: 484 (Col. Godwin's Report — Hoke's Brigade)

Hand-to-Hand Combat Amid Wiedrich's & Ricketts' Guns

OR 1: 457 (Col. Carroll's Brigade Report)
OR 1: 458-459 (Col. Coons' Report — 14th IN)
OR 1: 460 (Col. Carpenter's Report — 4th OH)
OR 1: 463-464 (Col. Lockwood's Report — 7th WV)
OR 1: 731 Gen. Schurz's Report) — The 58th NY and 119th NY were sent together to repulse the attack. Ironically, the 58th claimed they both arrived too late, but the 119th claimed they saved the day!? See the next two reports.
OR 1: 740 (Capt. Koenig's Report — 58th NY) — The attack "was repulsed before we arrived."
OR 1: 743 (Major Willis' Report — 119th NY) — Claimed that "in conjunction with the gallant Fifty-eighth, drove [the enemy] back, saved the position, and thus secured the whole army from irreparable disaster."
OR 1: 749 (Major Osborn's Artillery Report)
OR 1: 873 (Gen. Tyler's Artillery Report**) — Read about Ricketts' battery.
OR 1: 894 (Capt. Ricketts' Battery Report**)
OR 2: 486-487 (Maj. Tate's Report** — 6th NC) — Tate is clearly angry over not receiving support to keep the hill after his men captured the guns.

The Death Of Colonel Avery
  OR 2: 485 (Col. Godwin's Report — Hoke's Brigade)
  OR 2: 487 (Maj. Tate's Report — 6th NC)

Rodes' Failed Advance On The Right
  OR 2: 447 (Gen. Ewell's II Corps Report)
  OR 2: 556 (Gen. Rodes' Division Report**) — Claims Ramseur halted the advance.
  OR 2: 568 (Gen. Daniel's Brigade Report)
  OR 2: 573 (Col. Lewis' Report — 43rd NC)
  OR 2: 580 (Gen. Iverson's Brigade Report)
  OR 2: 582 (Gen. Doles' Brigade Report)
  OR 2: 585 (Col. Mercer's Report — 21st GA) — The advance occurred "after dark".
  OR 2: 586 (Maj. Peebles' Report — 44th GA) — Called it a "reconnaissance".
  OR 2: 587-588 (Gen. Ramseur's Brigade Report**) — Claimed Cemetery Hill was far too strong to attack with any chance of success.
  OR 2: 590 (Col. Grimes' Report — 4th NC)
  OR 2: 593 (Gen. O'Neal's Brigade Report)
  OR 2: 596 (Col. Hall's Report — 5th AL)
  OR 2: 659 (Maj. Engelhard's Report — Pender's Division)
  OR 2: 663 (Col. Perrin's Brigade Report**) — Read about Capt. Haskell's charge.
  OR 2: 666 (Gen. Lane's Brigade**)

Culp's Hill

Culp's Hill marked the right of Meade's army on July 2nd. There Major General Henry Slocum's 12th Corps had constructed a line of breastworks and trenches from the hill's summit down its south slope to Spangler's Spring. After Longstreet began his attack on Little Round Top, Meade called for reinforcements from Slocum. Slocum sent his 1st Division under Brigadier General Thomas Ruger and two brigades (Candy's and Kane's) of his 2nd Division under Brigadier General John Geary to support the Union left. This left only one brigade of "1350 men," commanded by 62-year old Brigadier General George Greene, behind breastworks along the crest of Culp's Hill and its upper south slope. To Greene's left was Wadsworth's Division to Steven's Knoll, but Greene's right was the problem. His line down upper Culp's Hill ended at a shallow ravine. The remainder of breastworks and trenches of the 1st Division, from the ravine all the way down lower Culp's Hill to Spangler's Spring, were temporarily vacant. But before Greene could extend his line, Confederates gained possession of the vacant intrenchments. It was Major General Edward Johnson's Division of Ewell's Corps, and they outnumbered Greene's men more than three-to-one. If they could take the summit, then the Confederates would have a commanding position from which to fire on the center of the Union line on Cemetery Hill and Ridge.

The Confederates "made four distinct charges" that evening against Greene's men, and all were repulsed. It was "an incessant attack" against "vastly superior numbers," reported General Geary. Greene did receive immediate assistance from six regiments of the 1st and 11th Corps, who alternated with his regiments to help them replenish exhausted ammunition, but "not more than 1300 men were in the lines at any one time." As General Kane later wrote, "the noble veteran Greene [fought a] resistance against overwhelming odds."

The fighting had started around 7:00 p.m. and lasted until about 10:00 p.m. At nightfall, the Confederates still possessed the entrenchments on lower Culp's Hill and had gained control of some of the ground west of them to a parallel stone wall fronting a field (later called Pardee Field). They would not push any farther in the darkness. Little did they know that the main Union supply trains were only several hundred yards away on the Baltimore Pike. But with the attack on the Union left over, Ruger's and Geary's men had been recalled back and soon began to return. Ruger's men had reached south Cemetery Ridge only after the fighting there was over, and Geary's men got lost on the way, so neither had yet seen action. But in the darkness, and unaware Confederates occupied their original entrenchments, the first of their troops to return were "met by a sharp fire" from the enemy. This sparked some brief skirmishing and a few soldiers were captured by both sides. "I devoted the rest of the night," wrote General Geary, "to [the] arrangement of my troops…for a vigorous attack at daylight to drive the enemy from the ground they had gained."

DESCRIPTION OF
OR 1: 773 (Gen. Williams' Division Report) — "a rocky and wooded ridge"
OR 1: 778 (Gen. Ruger's Report** — Williams' Division)
OR 1: 825 (Gen. Geary's Division Report**) — "a steep rocky mount"
OR 1: 849 (Col. Cobham's Report — Kane's Brigade)
OR 1: 855-856 (Gen. Greene's Brigade Report**)
OR 1: 870 (Lieut. Muhlenberg's Artillery Report)
OR 2: 504 (Gen. Johnson's Division Report**) — "a natural fortification"
OR 2: 532 (Gen. Jones' Brigade Report)

EVENING FIGHTING AGAINST GREENE'S BRIGADE
OR 1: 759-761 (Gen. Slocum's XII Corps Report**) — Be careful with map on p. 760
OR 1: 773-774 (Gen. Williams' Division Report**)
OR 1: 815 (Col. Fesler's Report — 27th IN) — Claims Ruger's men left for Little Round Top at 6 p.m.

OR 1: 816 (Col. Morse's Report — 2nd MA)
OR 1: 826-827 (Gen. Geary's Division Report**)
OR 1: 856-858 (Gen. Greene's Brigade Report**)
OR 1: 860-861 (Col. Godard's Report — 60th NY)
OR 1: 862 (Col. Redington's Report — 60th NY)
OR 1: 863 (Col. Hammerstein's Report — 78th NY)
OR 1: 864-865 (Col. Stegman's Report — 102nd NY)
OR 1: 866-867 (Col. Ireland's Report** — 137th NY) — Read about the bayonet charge of Captain Gregg.
OR 1: 868 (Col. Barnum's Report** — 149th NY)
OR 2: 504 (Gen. Johnson's Division Report)
OR 2: 509-510 (Gen. Steuart's Brigade Report)
OR 2: 513 (Col. Williams' Report — Nicholls' Brigade)
OR 2: 532 (Gen. Jones' Brigade Report)
OR 2: 533 (Col. Dungan's Report — 48th VA)
OR 2: 535 (Capt. Moseley's Report — 21st VA)
OR 2: 537 (Capt. Richardson's Report — 42nd VA) — Claims his regiment "got within 30 paces of the enemy's works".
OR 2: 538 (Capt. Buckner's Report** — 44th VA)
OR 2: 539 Col. Salyer's Report** — 50th VA)

CONFEDERATES OCCUPY UNION TRENCHES AND SPANGLER'S SPRING

OR 1: 780 (Gen. Ruger's Report** — Williams' Division) — See map on p. 779.
OR 1: 878 (Lieut. Gillett's Ordnance Report) — The close proximity of the Union ammunition train.
OR 2: 504 (Gen. Johnson's Division Report**) — It was Steuart's brigade who grabbed the vacant Union breastworks.
OR 2: 509-510 (Gen. Steuart's Brigade Report)

RUGER'S & GEARY'S MEN RETURN

OR 1: 778-780 (Gen. Ruger's Report** — Williams' Division) — Found the enemy in their breastworks.
OR 1: 783 (Col. McDougall's Brigade Report)
OR 1: 790-791 (Col. Packer's Report — 5th CT)
OR 1: 798 (Col. Rogers' Report — 123rd NY)
OR 1: 800 (Col. Price's Report — 145th NY)
OR 1: 813 (Col. Colgrove's Report — Ruger's Brigade)
OR 1: 816-817 (Col. Morse's Report** — 2nd MA) — They captured more than 20 Rebels in the night skirmish.
OR 1: 819-820 (Col. Crane's Report** — 107th NY) — Claims the skirmish occurred shortly after 10 p.m.
OR 1: 827 (Gen. Geary's Division Report**)
OR 1: 836 (Col. Candy's Brigade Report)

OR 1: 840-841 (Col. Creighton's Report — 7th OH)
OR 1: 847 (Gen. Kane's Brigade Report**) — In the darkness, Kane's men walked into a volley from the Confederates occupying their trenches.
OR 1: 849 (Col. Cobham's Report — Kane's Brigade)
OR 1: 851-852 (Col. Rickard's Report** — 29th PA)
OR 1: 853 (Capt. Gimber's Report — 109th PA)

Big Round Top

After the fighting on Little Round Top, Colonel James Rice, now in command of Vincent's Brigade, determined to take Big Round Top. The Alabamans and Texans who had been beaten back by Chamberlain's men still held its summit. As Chamberlain wrote, "if the enemy were allowed to strengthen himself in that position, he would have a great advantage in renewing the attack on us at daylight or before." At around 9:00 p.m., the 20th Maine (now numbering only 200 men) advanced up the mountain with bayonets fixed. They encountered little resistance and captured 25 Confederates as they took the crest. Men of Colonel Joseph Fisher's brigade reinforced them during the night, and there they remained until noon of the next day. Throughout the night, Chamberlain had his pickets report to him every half-hour because Confederates still remained just downslope of his position. As Chamberlain reported, the "enemy" was so near that "their movements and words [were] distinctly heard by us."

DESCRIPTION OF
OR 1: 531 (Gen. Humphrey's Division Report)

THE 20TH MAINE SEIZES BIG ROUND TOP
OR 1: 618 (Col. Rice's Report — Vincent's Brigade)
OR 1: 625-626 (Col. Chamberlain's Report** — 20th ME) — Chamberlain claims Colonel Fisher's brigade was no help in taking Big Round Top.
OR 1: 654 (Gen. Crawford's Division Report) — Crawford's report disagrees with Chamberlain's over Fisher's brigade.
OR 1: 658 (Col. Fisher's Brigade Report) — Fisher's claims of taking Big Round Top seem exaggerated.

The Leister Farmhouse

Meade held a council with his corps and wing commanders at his headquarters in the evening of July 2nd. The place was a small farmhouse owned by a widow, Lydia Leister, and situated on the Taneytown Road behind the center of Hancock's lines on Cemetery Ridge. It was about 9:00 p.m. when they gathered, and the fighting on Culp's Hill was still going on. For several hours, in a hot and cramped room of the house, they discussed the number of troops left, the need for supplies, the strengths and weaknesses of their battle position, and strategy. Eventually, they held a vote on what to do. Each of the nine generals present gave his opinion, and Slocum was the last to reply. "Stay and fight it out," he said. Three had advocated modifying the army's present position, but all concurred in remaining at Gettysburg. Meade agreed with them firmly. In fact, staying was not the issue because he had earlier sent a telegram to Washington that he would "remain in his present position." He mainly called for the council to ascertain the army's condition as he decided whether or not to attack or sit tight the next day. On this matter, his generals wanted to wait and see if Lee would attack, and Meade concurred. The meeting ended shortly before midnight, and they dispersed to their respective commands to prepare for the morrow's fighting.

THE COUNCIL OF WAR
  OR 1: 72-73 (Gen. Meade's Report)

4

The Third Day

"The angel of death alone can produce such a field as was presented."

The Angle, shown here in this 1882 photograph for visiting artist Paul Philippoteaux, is where the Union army repulsed Pickett's Charge on July 3, 1863. It was the largest attack at Gettysburg, and became the subject of the greatest cyclorama ever painted. The fields were littered with more than 6,000 dead and wounded. This chapter is devoted to providing the battle reports and parts of those reports that discuss the combat of the third day. Included herein are the fighting at Culp's Hill, the great cannonade (which more soldiers commented about than any other battle event), Pickett's Charge, the Wheatfield, and the final engagements between Union and Confederate cavalry.

Culp's Hill

The fight for Culp's Hill resumed just before dawn on July 3rd, and it lasted for seven hours. This was the longest uninterrupted engagement of the entire battle.

Around 4:00 a.m., two batteries of Union guns west of the Baltimore Pike opened against the Confederate lines and "fired for fifteen minutes without intermission." Then upon the "discontinuance of the fire," wrote Brigadier General Alpheus Williams, "the enemy…attacked…with great fury." It would be the first of three major Confederate assaults against the hill. The first two assaults were aimed against the crest and upper south slope of Culp's Hill where Greene's Brigade remained firm. During the night, the rest of Geary's Division had reinforced Greene's flanks, and on Greene's far left, up on the very summit of the hill, stood the 66th Ohio. Upon orders, they daringly advanced outside of the breastworks, exposing themselves to both enemy and friendly-fire. They formed a line perpendicular to Greene's that had them facing south and proceeded to "harass the enemy by an enfilading fire" all morning long.

By 10:00 a.m., Confederate General Johnson ordered a final all-out attack along his entire line from Spangler's Spring up Culp's Hill. He positioned Brigadier General James Walker's "Stonewall" brigade to strike against Greene's troops. Again the assault failed, but not for lack of courage. Against the summit, Walker's men endured "a murderous and enfilading fire" for "some three-quarters of an hour," and some of his troops had "advanced so far up the side of the hill [to] the enemy's defenses" that when "the regiments in support gave way" many of them were captured. Walker ordered his brigade to fall back because "it was a useless sacrifice of life to keep them longer under so galling a fire."

FEDERAL GUNS OPEN THE BATTLE
 OR 1: 791 (Col. Packer's Report — 5th CT) — Union artillery opened at 4 a.m.
 OR 1: 800 (Col. Price's Report — 145th NY) — Union artillery opened at 4 a.m.
 OR 1: 818 (Col. Grimes' Report — 13th NJ)
 OR 1: 870-871 (Lieut Muhlenberg's Artillery Report**) — Rugg's and Kinsie's batteries open the morning fight.
 OR 1: 873 (Gen. Tyler's Artillery Report) — Read about Rigby's battery.
 OR 1: 899 (Capt. Rigby's Battery Report)

Morning Fight Against Greene's Brigade

OR 1: 682-683 (Gen. Shaler's Brigade Report)
OR 1: 761 (Gen. Slocum's XII Corps Report**)
OR 1: 775 (Gen. Williams' Division Report**)
OR 1: 780-781 (Gen. Ruger's Report — Williams' Division)
OR 1: 805 (Gen. Lockwood's Brigade Report)
OR 1: 808-809 (Col. Wallace's Report — 1st MD Eastern Shore)
OR 1: 810 (Col. Ketchum's Report — 150th NY) — "the large number of dead."
OR 1: 827-831 (Gen. Geary's Division Report**) — Read about the 66th Ohio and CSA Major Leigh.
OR 1: 836-837 (Col. Candy's Brigade Report**) — Highlights the 66th Ohio.
OR 1: 841 (Col. Creighton's Report** — 7th OH) — How Union regiments alternated at the front, and of Confederate surrender and CSA Major Leigh.
OR 1: 843 (Capt. Hayes' Report — 29th OH) — Confederates wave flag of truce.
OR 1: 844 (Col. Powell's Report — 66th OH)
OR 1: 847 (Gen. Kane's Brigade Report**)
OR 1: 849 (Col. Cobham's Report** — Kane's Brigade)
OR 1: 852 (Col. Rickards' Report — 29th PA)
OR 1: 853 (Capt. Gimber's Report — 109th PA)
OR 1: 854-855 (Col. Walker's Report — 111th PA)
OR 1: 857-858 (Gen. Greene's Brigade Report**) — See numbers and losses, p. 858.
OR 1: 861 (Col. Godard's Report — 60th NY)
OR 1: 863 (Col. Hammerstein's Report — 78th NY)
OR 1: 865 (Col. Stegman's Report — 102nd NY)
OR 1: 867 (Col. Ireland's Report — 137th NY)
OR 1: 868 (Col. Barnum's Report — 149th NY) — Flag pierced by 81 balls!
OR 2: 504 (Gen. Johnson's Division Report)
OR 2: 513 (Col. Williams' Report — Nicholls' Brigade) — His men were engaged for hours "without cessation".
OR 2: 519 (Gen. Walker's Report — Stonewall Brigade)
OR 2: 521-522 (Col. Nadenbousch's Report — 2nd VA)
OR 2: 523 (Maj. Terry's Report — 4th VA) — They attacked the summit, "fortified with earthworks and abatis [sic]," and took a heavy loss in prisoners.
OR 2: 526 (Col. Funk's Report — 5th VA)
OR 2: 528 (Col. Shriver's Report — 27th VA)
OR 2: 530 (Capt. Golladay's Report — 33rd VA)
OR 2: 593 (Col. O'Neal's Brigade Report)
OR 2: 595 (Col. Battle's Report — 3rd AL)
OR 2: 600 (Capt. Bowie's Report — 6th AL)
OR 2: 601 (Col. Pickens' Report — 12th AL)

Pardee Field, Spangler's Spring & Meadow

Shortly after the Union guns opened the fight on Culp's Hill, Lieutentant Colonel Ario Pardee's 147th Pennsylvania regiment was ordered forward. They charged and occupied a stone wall on the west edge of a field (later named in honor of Pardee). Across it they fired obliquely on the Confederates in the trenches, and along with the 20th Connecticut and some other key regiments, they fought off any Confederate attempt to advance across the field and flank the Union right on Culp's Hill. The 20th Connecticut was positioned in the woods on the south edge of Pardee's field. There they were midway between Union artillery behind them and the entrenched Confederates in their front. For "over five hours" the 20th engaged advancing Confederates in order to keep them "in check" while also informing Union artillery as to the "range of the enemy" in order to shell them in the trenches. It was a hazardous job. Union Colonel Archibald McDougall observed, "the farther [the 20th Connecticut] pushed the enemy, the more directly [they were] placed under the fire of our own guns." Indeed, some of the regiment were hit by the Union artillery fire they were trying to direct.

In the trenches were the Confederates of Brigadier General George Steuart's Brigade. When General Johnson ordered the third and massive assault against Culp's Hill around 10:00 a.m., Steuart's men came out of the trenches and attacked across Pardee Field against the 147th Pennsylvania and other Union troops guarding the Federal right on Culp's Hill. The head-on charge across open terrain exposed them to a raking cross-fire from Union artillery and infantry. Steuart saw his line crumble and he was forced to withdraw his men to avoid "total annihilation."

After the repulse, the 2nd Massachusetts and the 27th Indiana regiments were ordered "by mistake" to countercharge from their position in McAllister's Woods across the "swale" of Spangler's Meadow against the Confederate left flank and force the rebels from the trenches of lower Culp's Hill. There a fresh Confederate brigade was waiting, and the Union loss was ghastly. The 2nd Massachusetts lost 130 men in the charge alone. "The two regiments were devoted to destruction," observed Colonel Silas Colgrove, but "scarcely a man could live to gain the position of the enemy," and he ordered the regiments back.

The Confederates' position in the entrenchments was too hot. Finding themselves under unrelenting fire from three sides by Union infantry and artillery, the Southerners retired from the breastworks or surrendered. "As they fell back," wrote General Geary, "our troops rushed forward with wild cheers of victory, driving the rebels in confusion over the entrenchments." Many Confederates were captured in the trenches, and some raised white flags. It was around 11:00 a.m., and as Johnson withdrew his division back to Rock Creek, the scene of carnage left behind from "seven hours [of] unremitting fury" was sobering. "The heaps and mounds of dead and wounded which were found...," wrote Union Colonel William Mausby, "might well satisfy the ambition for bloody deeds of each man of every regiment engaged, however craving such ambition might be."

DESCRIPTION OF
OR 1: 778-779 (Gen. Ruger's Report) — Describes area, see map.
No official report from either army mentions the name "Spangler's Spring."

THE FIRST MARYLAND POTOMAC STRIKES FIRST AT SPANGLER'S SPRING
OR 1: 804 (Gen. Lockwood's Brigade Report)
OR 1: 806-807 (Col. Mausby's Report — 1st MD Potomac)
OR 1: 820 (Col. Crane's Report — 107th NY) — Read about the 1st Maryland Potomac's advance.

FIGHTING ACROSS PARDEE FIELD
OR 1: 793-794 (Col. Wooster's Report — 20th CT)
OR 1: 827-831 (Gen. Geary's Division Report) — The charge of the 147th PA.
OR 1: 836 (Col. Candy's Brigade Report) — The charge of 147th PA.
OR 1: 839-840 (Col. Patrick's Report — 5th OH)
OR 1: 845-846 (Col. Pardee's Report** — 147th PA)
OR 2: 511 (Gen. Steuart's Brigade Report) — "The enemy's position was impregnable..."
OR 2: 568-569 (Gen. Daniel's Brigade Report) — His brigade attacked Union breastworks to support Steuart's charge across Pardee Field.
OR 2: 572 (Col. Brabble's Report — 32nd NC)
OR 2: 573 (Col. Lewis' Report — 43rd NC)
OR 2: 575 (Capt. Hopkins' Report** — 45th NC) — Claims that in the span of "about five minutes...we killed more than in all our fighting before or after."

CHARGE OF THE 2ND MASSACHUSETTS AND 27TH INDIANA
OR 1: 781 (Gen. Ruger's Report** — Williams' Division) — Explains the order to charge was misunderstood. See map on p. 779 for the "swale."
OR 1: 813-814 (Col. Colgrove's Report** — Ruger's Brigade)
OR 1: 815 (Col. Fesler's Report — 27th IN)
OR 1: 817 (Col. Morse's Report** — 2nd MA)

DRIVING THE CONFEDERATES OUT OF THE TRENCHES
OR 1: 781 (Gen. Ruger's Report — Williams' Division) — See map on p. 779. Mistakenly claims 123rd New York led division in pushing Confederates out of the breastworks. See McDougall's report.

OR 1: 784 (Col. McDougall's Brigade Report) — Highlights actions of 20th Connecticut, and claims 123rd New York entered breastworks after Confederates were long gone.
OR 1: 793-794 (Col. Wooster's Report** — 20th CT)
OR 1: 798 (Col. Rogers' Report** — 123rd NY)
OR 1: 806 (Col. Mausby's Report — 1st MD Potomac)
OR 1: 824 (Col. Hawley's Report — 3rd WI) — The fight ended about 11:00 a.m.
OR 1: 827-831 (Gen. Geary's Division Report**) — The First Maryland, CSA, made the last Confederate charge against Culp's Hill that morning.
OR 1: 840 (Col. Patrick's Report — 5th OH)
OR 2: 511 (Gen. Steuart's Brigade Report)
OR 2: 573-574 (Col. Lewis' Report — 43rd NC)
OR 2: 575 (Capt. Hopkins' Report — 45th NC)

CONFEDERATES SKIRMISH WITH THE FEDERALS INTO THE NIGHT
OR 1: 785 (Col. McDougall's Brigade Report)
OR 1: 801 (Col. Price's Report — 145th OH)
OR 1: 840 (Col. Patrick's Report — 5th OH) — Observed some Confederate sharpshooters had "air rifles".
OR 2: 569 (Gen. Daniel's Brigade Report) — Skirmishers engaged from 3 p.m. until nearly midnight.

Wolf Hill

Wolf Hill is situated south of Spangler's Spring across from Rock Creek and covered by pasture and open woods. In the mid-morning of July 3rd, Brigadier General Thomas Neill's Brigade of the Union 6th Corps was ordered there to hold "the extreme right of the whole army, and prevent the enemy from turning us." After the first two regiments of the brigade arrived on its summit and positioned themselves to face north, they encountered several companies of Confederate sharpshooters from Johnson's Division who had crossed Rock Creek to determine the extent of Union lines and keep the Confederate "left flank clear." Skirmishing went back and forth all day until the Confederates finally withdrew. Neill's men suffered just 14 casualties, but they held an important position that is often overlooked today.

NEILL'S BRIGADE HOLDS THE EXTREME RIGHT OF THE UNION ARMY
OR 1: 675 (Gen. Howe's Division Report)
OR 1: 680 (Gen. Neill's Brigade Report)
OR 1: 779 (Gen. Ruger's Report — Williams' Division)
OR 2: 521-522 (Col. Nadenbousch's Report — 2nd VA)

Town of Gettysburg

Skirmishing between Confederate sharpshooters in the south end of town and Union troops on the north side of Cemetery Hill had occurred continuously since the evening of July 1st. The troops most vulnerable to being picked-off were the Union artillerists manning their guns atop the summit of Cemetery Hill. But on July 3rd, Gettysburg's only civilian casualty was killed in the crossfire. That morning, a company of Union soldiers had occupied several houses situated along the Baltimore Pike near the base of Cemetery Hill. According to Union Captain Emil Koenig, "the enemy's sharpshooters kept up a brisk fire at these houses, and killed a girl who was living in one of them." Her name was Virginia Wade, and she was 20 years old. A minie ball had struck her through the front door of her sister's home. Men of the 58th New York infantry occupied the house for the remainder of the battle, but none were ever harmed even though the house itself "was completely pierced by bomb-shells and rifle-balls." A few days later, the young woman was buried by her family in the yard behind the house. Six months afterward, her body was removed to the German Reformed Church cemetery, but she was reinterred again in 1865 to the town's Evergreen Cemetery on Cemetery Hill where her grave is today.

THE KILLING OF "JENNIE" WADE
   OR 1: 741 (Capt. Koenig's Report — 58th NY)

SKIRMISHING BETWEEN TOWN AND CEMETERY HILL
   OR 1: 715 (Col. Harris' Report — 75th OH)
   OR 1: 718-719 (Maj. Brady's Report — 17th CT)
   OR 1: 722 (Gen. Steinwehr's Division Report)
   OR 1: 724 (Col. Smith's Brigade Report)
   OR 1: 726 (Col. Wood's Report — 136th NY)
   OR 1: 741 (Capt. Koenig's Report — 58th NY)
   OR 1: 752 (Capt. Wiedrich's Battery Report)
   OR 2: 598 (Maj. Blackford's Report — Battalion of Sharpshooters)

CONFEDERATES GUARDING THE STREETS OF GETTYSBURG
   OR 2: 596 (Col. Hall's Report — 5th AL)

Seminary Ridge and the Bliss Farm

General Lee's original battle plan for July 3rd was "unchanged" from the previous day. "Longstreet…was ordered to attack the next morning, and General Ewell was directed to assail the enemy's right at the same time," wrote Lee in his report. But by the morning of July

3rd, Lee knew that his generals were unable to attack in concert. While Ewell's forces under Johnson were heavily engaged with the Union right on Culp's Hill, Longstreet had yet to launch his attack on the Union left. Having ridden over Seminary Ridge to see Longstreet, and finding him so "delayed," Lee decided on an "assault to be made directly at the enemy's main position, the Cemetery Hill." Longstreet's fresh division under Major General George Pickett would lead it, along with Heth's Division (under Pettigrew's command) and portions of Pender's (under Major General Isaac Trimble's command), across the nearly mile wide fields that separated Seminary Ridge from Cemetery Ridge. Lee also planned to have Longstreet's, Hill's, and Ewell's artillery "open simultaneously...to silence those [guns] of the enemy...and the assaulting column [would then] advance under cover of [their] combined fire." But Longstreet firmly disagreed, believing "the distance to be passed over...and in plain view, seemed too great to insure great results..." against Meade's army.

Meanwhile that morning, Confederate batteries at the Peach Orchard engaged Union skirmish lines that had advanced to retake the ravine of Plum Run and the woods along it. Also Confederate Whitworth guns were removed from Seminary Ridge to Oak Ridge from where they could enfilade the Union line from Cemetery Hill on down Cemetery Ridge to Little Round Top. According to Colonel Thomas Smyth on Cemetery Ridge, skirmishing between Union and Confederate artillery and infantry "continued all along the line until 10:30 a.m., when a lull ensued."

The skirmishing that most annoyed Union troops on Cemetery Ridge came from the Bliss house and barn. Union forces had twice dislodged "the enemy's sharpshooters" from the buildings on July 2nd, but Confederate skirmishers were back in them again. Union Brigadier General Alexander Hays sent orders to retake the buildings and burn them, which the 14th Connecticut promptly carried out "in the forenoon" of the day. No building now stood between Hays' troops on Cemetery Ridge and the Confederates on Seminary Ridge.

At about 1:00 p.m., two Confederate guns from Major Benjamin Eshleman's artillery positioned at the Peach Orchard opened fire "in quick succession" to signal the start of the cannonade. Immediately all Confederate guns along Seminary Ridge opened "simultaneously upon the enemy...," observed Major Eshleman, "and a most terrific artillery duel ensued." Over 220 Union and Confederate cannon raged back and forth for nearly two hours. As Union Lieutenant Colonel Freeman McGilvery observed, "the enemy...[fired] upon our lines with at least one hundred and forty guns." In return, Union artillery responded with about 80 guns. Surprisingly, relatively few casualties were incurred on either side. Confederate projectiles passed "from 20-100 feet over our lines," reported Colonel McGilvery. Union guns were no more successful, and ammunition needed to be conserved. "About 2:30 p.m., finding our ammunition running low," wrote Union General and Chief-of-Artillery Henry Hunt, "I directed that the fire should be gradually stopped, which was done, and the enemy soon slackened his fire also."

The cannonade would be commented on in more officer's reports than any other event of the battle. No other battle event was ever witnessed by everyone, but everyone heard the cannonade, and it was astounding to all. As Confederate Brigadier General and Chief-of-Artillery William Pendleton later reflected upon it, "so mighty an artillery contest has perhaps never been waged."

LEE PLANS A NEW ATTACK: LEE-LONGSTREET CONTROVERSY
OR 2: 308 & 320 (Gen. Lee's Reports**)
OR 2: 359 (Gen. Longstreet's Report**)
OR 2: 620 (Gen. Wilcox's Report**) — Wilcox observes that Union cannon were not disabled by the cannonade, thereby indirectly supporting Longstreet's opinion that the charge would be difficult.

MORNING SKIRMISHING
OR 1: 417 (Gen. Gibbon's Division Report)
OR 1: 465 (Col. Smyth's Brigade Report)
OR 2: 434 & 436 (Maj. Eschleman's Battalion Report**) — Read about Forrest and Brown's capture of an abandoned union gun while under fire.
OR 2: 663 (Col. Perrin's Brigade Report**)
OR 2: 666 (Gen. Lane's Brigade Report)
OR 2: 673-674 (Maj. Poague's Battalion Report)
OR 2: 674-675 (Maj. McIntosh's Battalion Report**) — Mentions Whitworths.

BURNING THE BLISS FARM
OR 1: 465 (Col. Smyth's Brigade Report**)
OR 1: 467 (Maj. Ellis' Report** — 14th CT)
OR 1: 470 (Major Hill's Report — 12th NJ)

THE CANNONADE: CEMETERY RIDGE UNDER FIRE
OR 1: 239 & 240 (Gen. Hunt's Artillery Report**)
OR 1: 316 (Col. Biddle's Report — 121st PA)
OR 1: 318 & 322 (Col. Gates' Report — 20th NYS Militia / 80th NY)
OR 1: 372-373 (Gen. Hancock's II Corps Report)
OR 1: 380 (Gen. Caldwell's Division Report) — "the most fearful fire I have ever witnessed"

OR 1: 382 (Col. McKeen's Report — Cross' Brigade) — "... a terrible fire, which, however, did the brigade but little injury ..."
OR 1: 383 (Maj. Cross' Report — 5th NH)
OR 1: 385 (Col. Broady's Report — 61st NY)
OR 1: 386 (Col. Kelly's Brigade Report) — "the heaviest artillery fire ever heard"
OR 1: 387 (Col. Richard Brynes Report — 28th MA)
OR 1: 388 (Capt. Touhy's Report — 63rd NY)
OR 1: 391 (Capt. Burke's Report — 88th NY)
OR 1: 392 (Col. Mulholland's Report — 116th PA)
OR 1: 395 (Col. Fraser's Report — Zook's Brigade) — "The severe and long-continued artillery fire ... inflicted no loss on the brigade."
OR 1: 396 (Capt. Sherrer's Report — 52nd NY)
OR 1: 397 (Col. Chapman's Report – 57th NY) — "the most severe and long-continued artillery fire of the war"
OR 1: 410 (Col. McMichael's Report — 53rd PA)
OR 1: 417 (Gen. Gibbon's Division Report) — Claims it lasted two hours.
OR 1: 420 (Gen. Harrow's Division Report) — Claims the cannonade lasted from 1 p.m. to "nearly 3 p.m."
OR 1: 425 (Capt. Coates' Report — 1st MN)
OR 1: 426 (Capt. Darrow's Report — 82nd NY) — "we lost a number of men during the cannonade."
OR 1: 428 (Gen. Webb's Brigade Report)
OR 1: 431 (Capt. Davis' Report — 69th PA)
OR 1: 437 (Col. Hall's Brigade Report**) — "The experience…can never be forgotten by those who survived it."
OR 1: 443 (Col. Devereux's Report) — "The most terrific cannonading of the war."
OR 1: 445 (Capt. Abbott's Report — 20th MA)
OR 1: 448 & 449 (Maj. Curtis' Report — 7th MI) — "Nearly all the shot and shell struck in front and ricocheted over us, or passed over us and burst in our rear."
OR 1: 451 (Col. Mallon's Report — 42nd NY)
OR 1: 452 (Capt. McFadden's Report — 59th NY)
OR 1: 454 (Gen. Hays' Division Report**)
OR 1: 461 (Col. Sawyer's Report — 8th OH)
OR 1: 473 (Col. Bull's Report — Willard's Brigade)
OR 1: 476 (Capt. Seeley's Report — 111th NY) — "[The] cannonading and shelling [was] unparalleled, it is believed, in warfare."
OR 1: 478-480 (Capt. Hazard's Artillery Report**)
OR 1: 489 (Gen. French's Report**) — He was miles away and "heard the cannon at Gettysburg on July 3."
OR 1: 706 (Gen. Howard's XI Corps Report)
OR 1: 722 (Gen. Steinwehr's Division Report) — Cannonade was directed against Cemetery Hill.

OR 1: 736 (Col. Dobke's Report — 45th NY)
OR 1: 745 (Maj. Ledig's Report — 75th PA)
OR 1: 750 (Major Osborn's Artillery Report)
OR 1: 784-785 (Col. McDougall's Brigade Report)
OR 1: 871 (Lieut. Muhlenberg's Artillery Report)
OR 1: 874-875 (Gen. Tyler's Artillery Report) — Cannonade pounds Union artillery reserve. Read about Private Sheridan.
OR 1: 878-879 (Lieut. Gillett's Ordnance Report**) — Cannonade strikes Union ammunition train.
OR 1: 883-884 (Col. McGilvery's Artillery Report**)
OR 1: 885 (Capt. Phillips' Battery Report**) — Hunt's and Hancock's conflicting orders.
OR 1: 888 (Capt. Hart's Battery Report**)
OR 1: 889 (Lieut. McMahon's Report — Hart's Battery)
OR 1: 892-893 (Capt. Edgell's Battery Report)
OR 1: 1042 (Col. Veazey's Report — 16th VT)
OR 2: 352 Gen. Pendleton's Report**) — Nearly 150 opened fire.
OR 2: 375-376 (Col. Cabell's Battalion Report) — Artillery posted en echelon.
OR 2: 380-381 (Capt. Manly's Battery Report) — Fired from the Peach Orchard.
OR 2: 385 (Maj. Peyton's Report — Garnett's Brigade)
OR 2: 388-389 (Maj. Dearing's Battalion Report**) — Union guns went silent.
OR 2: 430 (Col. E. P. Alexander's Battalion Report) — He makes no mention of the Cannonade or Pickett's Charge in his report!
OR 2: 434-435 (Maj. Eshleman's Battalion Report**) — His guns open the duel!
OR 2: 557 (Gen. Rodes' Division Report**) — Rodes proclaimed it "the fiercest and grandest cannonade I have ever witnessed."
OR 2: 603 (Col. Carter's Battalion Report)
OR 2: 604 (Capt. Dance's Battalion Report) — Carter's and Dance's guns were posted immediately left and right of the Railroad Cut on Oak Ridge from which they fired at the Union guns on Cemetery Hill before and during Longstreet's assault.
OR 2: 608 (Gen. Hill's III Corps Report)
OR 2: 610 (Col. Walker's Artillery Report)
OR 2: 614-615 (Gen. Anderson's Division Report) — Wilcox's Brigade suffered severely from the cannonade.
OR 2: 619-620 (Gen. Wilcox's Brigade Report**)
OR 2: 632 (Col. Lang's Brigade Report)
OR 2: 650-651 (Gen. Davis' Brigade Report)
OR 2: 675 (Maj. McIntosh's Battalion Report) — Fired Whitworth guns from Oak Hill.
OR 2: 678 (Capt. Brunson's Report** — Pegram's Battalion)

Pickett's Charge: The Pickett-Pettigrew Assault

After "the enemy ceased firing," wrote General Meade, "soon his masses of infantry became visible, forming for an assault on our left and left center." As the smoke from the cannonade cleared away, the Federals on Cemetery Ridge saw vast numbers of Confederates emerging from the woods of Seminary Ridge. The "time had arrived for the attack, and I gave the order to General Pickett to advance to the assault," reported General Longstreet, "[but] the order for this attack…would have been revoked had I felt that I had that privilege."

The Confederates making the assault faced "an open field in front, about three-quarters of a mile in width." They would cross the open ground in two columns. Pickett's Division (Kemper's, Garnett's, and Armistead's Brigades) would guide the attack on the right, with two brigades (Wilcox's and Lang's) in support guarding their right flank. Pettigrew's Division (Fry's, Marshall's, Davis', and Brockenbrough's Brigades) would march from the left, along with two brigades (Lowrance's & Lane's) in support commanded by Major General Trimble. They were to converge upon north Cemetery Ridge between the Copse of Trees and Ziegler's Grove where the Federals of Hancock's 2nd Corps waited behind a stone wall and fence. In the middle, the wall formed an angle, and was a weak point in the Union line. It was against this "salient" that Pickett and Pettigrew were to strike "at the same moment."

At about 3:00 p.m., the Confederate assault began and the troops advanced in a formation of three lines, totaling roughly 13,000 men. "The spectacle was magnificent," wrote one Union officer, who observed that the advancing rebels extended "across the plain for more than a mile." But it was not long before Union guns from Cemetery Hill all the way down Cemetery Ridge opened a hail of artillery fire that created great gaps in the Confederate ranks. Sometimes "as many as ten men were killed and wounded by the bursting of a single shell." As one Union officer observed, within "a few minutes, instead of a well-ordered line of battle, there were broken and confused masses." Unfortunately, the cannonade had so exhausted Confederate ammunition that Lee's artillery could not "render the necessary support" as originally planned. Worse, Pickett and Pettigrew's men had to climb over several fences in their crossing, which further slowed and exposed them to fire. When they climbed over the fence along the Emmitsburg Road, the Union artillery and infantry opened fire on the southerners, pouring grape, canister, and musketry into them. In the words of one Confederate officer, "the line moved forward…exposed to a murderous artillery and infantry fire in front, a severe artillery fire from the right, and an enfilade fire of musketry from the left." The survivors who pressed on headed for the stone wall at the Angle.

DESCRIPTION OF THE FIELDS
    OR 1: 437 (Col. Hall's Brigade Report)
    OR 2: 614 (Gen. Anderson's Division Report**)

THE TARGET OF THE CHARGE
    OR 2: 321 (Gen. Lee's Report) — The "enemy's left center."
    OR 2: 359 (Gen. Longstreet's I Corps Report) — Cemetery Hill.

WITNESS TO THE CHARGE
    OR 1: 318-319 (Col. Gates' Report** — 20th NYS Militia / 80th NY) — The "design" of the attack "was to break through our left center" (p. 319).
    OR 1: 373 (Gen. Hancock's II Corps Report)
    OR 1: 392-393 (Col. Mulholland's Report — 116th PA)
    OR 1: 417 (Gen. Gibbon's Division Report)
    OR 1: 420 (Gen. Harrow's Report — Gibbon's Division)
    OR 1: 437-439 (Col. Hall's Brigade Report**) — See map on p. 438.
    OR 1: 448 (Maj. Curtis' Report — 7th MI) — Noticed smoke had cleared away.
    OR 1: 454 (Gen. Hays' Division Report) — His troops began firing when the enemy approached within 100 yards.
    OR 1: 467 (Maj. Ellis' Report** — 14th CT)
    OR 1: 473 (Col. Bull's Report — Willard's Brigade) — The enemy advanced "in four lines across the flat" plain.
    OR 1: 476 (Capt. Seeley's Report — 111th NY) — The enemy advanced "in three heavy compact lines, preceded by a cloud of skirmishers."
    OR 1: 480-481 (Capt. Hazard's Artillery Report** — A shell lodged in the muzzle of one of Brown's battery guns on July 3 near the Copse of Trees.
    OR 1: 884 (Col. McGilvery's Artillery Report**)
    OR 1: 889 (Lieut. McMahon's Report — Hart's Battery)
    OR 2: 359-360 (Gen. Longstreet's I Corps Report**)
    OR 2: 385-387 (Maj. Peyton's Report** — Garnett's Brigade) — Confederates had to climb three post and rail fences as they crossed the fields (the third fence being at the Emmitsburg Road). Also read about Capt. Spessard's heroics on p. 387.
    OR 2: 435 (Maj. Eshleman's Battalion Report)
    OR 2: 608 (Gen. Hill's III Corps Report)
    OR 2: 614-615 (Gen. Anderson's Division Report**)
    OR 2: 620 (Gen. Wilcox's Brigade Report**)
    OR 2: 643-644 (Maj. Jones' Report** — 26th NC) — Losses were so severe that Marshall's (formerly Pettigrew's) brigade was left with one field officer! "Regiments that went in with colonels came out commanded by lieutenants."

OR 2: 647 (Col. Shepard's Report** — Fry's Brigade) — The "stout post and plank fences" along Emmitsburg Road "was a very great obstruction to us."
OR 2: 651 (Gen. Davis' Brigade Report**)
OR 2: 659-660 (Maj. Engelhard's Report — Pender's Division) — Report of Trimble's two brigades.
OR 2: 666 (Gen. Lane's Brigade Report)
OR 2: 671-672 (Col. Lowrance's Report** — Scales' Brigade) — "Then we were ordered forward over a wide, hot, and already crimson plain."

UNION CANNON FIRE DIRECTED AGAINST THE CHARGE
OR 1: 750 (Major Osborn's Artillery Report)
OR 1: 884 (Col. McGilvery's Artillery Report**)
OR 1: 888 (Capt. Hart's Battery Report)
OR 1: 889 (Lieut. McMahon's Report — Hart's Battery)
OR 1: 891 (Capt. Taft's Battery Report**)
OR 1: 892-893 (Capt. Edgell's Battery Report**) — Taft's and Edgell's batteries fired north and west from Cemetery Hill, demonstrating the pivotal importance of this height which commanded all parts of the Confederate lines.
OR 1: 898 (Lieut. Dow's Battery Report)
OR 1: 901 (Capt. Ames' Battery Report)
OR 1: 1021 (Capt. Robertson's Artillery Report)
OR 1: 1023 (Capt. Daniels' Report — 9th MI) — Ceased firing at 5:30 p.m.
OR 2: 386 (Maj. Peyton's Report — Garnett's Brigade) — Claims one Union battery on Little Round Top "enfiladed nearly our entire line".
OR 2: 620 (Gen. Wilcox's Brigade Report**) — The smoke of battle severely obscured visibility! Marching behind and in support of Pickett's Division, Wilcox claimed the smoke from Union artillery was so heavy that "not a man of the division that I was ordered to support could I see" (p. 620).
OR 2: 644 (Maj. Jones' Report — Marshall's Brigade)

CONFEDERATE CANNON FIRE TO SUPPORT THE CHARGE
OR 1: 319 (Col. Gates' Report — 20th NYS Militia/80th NY) — Observed that the Confederate batteries did "as much damage in their own ranks as in ours."
OR 2: 384 (Lieut. Motes' Report — Carlton's Battery)
OR 2: 389 (Maj. Dearing's Battalion Report)
OR 2: 435 (Maj. Eshleman's Battalion Report)
OR 2: 456 (Col. Brown's Artillery Report**) — Read why his battalions had to use solid shot.

The Angle and the Copse of Trees

From where the 1st Delaware Infantry stood, midway between the Copse of Trees and Ziegler's Grove, they saw the assaulting columns of Confederates come together in final attack. We "received the united attack of the Pickett and [Pettigrew] columns," wrote Lieutenant John Dent of the regiment, "...the Picket column moving on us in an oblique direction from the left, the [Pettigrew] column moving on us in an oblique direction from the right, both columns converging in our immediate front." Along their position with General Hays' Division, where the stone wall was set back, no Confederates ever pierced their lines. Instead, the main Confederate breakthrough occurred just a few dozen yards to their south, where the stone wall angled out and down to a copse of trees, defended mostly by two regiments of Brigadier General Alexander Webb's Brigade.

As Lee watched the grand assault from Seminary Ridge, he saw its left "waver" and then "finally [give] way." The 8th Ohio repelled Brockenbrough's Brigade and Union artillery and infantry under General Hays' command subsequently murdered the left and front of Pettigrew's and Trimble's advance. Union General Hancock saw the success his Corps had against the Confederate left. "In front of Hays' division it was not of very long duration...the enemy broke in great disorder, leaving fifteen colors and nearly 2000 prisoners." Meanwhile, on the right of the Confederate assault, Pickett's Division was fired on by Brigadier General William Harrow's and Colonel Norman Hall's Brigades, and Pickett's right flank was struck by regiments of Brigadier General George Stannard's Vermont Brigade. As Hancock later described it, the combined strikes against the Confederate left and right had a funneling effect that concentrated the main assault "opposite the brigade of General Webb" at the Angle and the Copse of Trees.

The Confederates approaching the stone wall and fence at the Angle were mostly of the brigades of Brigadier Generals Lewis Armistead and Richard Garnett, and there they met Webb's 69th and 71st regiments and Lieutenant Alonzo Cushing's battery. Cushing's bravery at this moment was exceptional. "Severely wounded [in both legs,]...he pushed [a] gun to the fence in front, and was killed [while] serving his last canister into the ranks of the advancing enemy." But the Confederates "advanced steadily to the fence," recalled General Webb, "driving out a portion of the Seventy-first Pennsylvania Volunteers." From Hancock's perspective, the "enemy [was] emboldened by seeing this indication of weakness...[and] pushed forward...crossing the breastwork abandoned by the troops." Webb watched in horror as "General Armistead passed over the fence with probably over 100 of his command." The situation was desperate. In the words of several Union officers, "the enemy was pouring over the rails..." and their "battle-flags were seen waving on the stone wall."

Stunned by the "crowd" of Armistead's men, the Union line at the Angle had been pushed back but it did not retreat, and "it remained in this way for about 10 minutes" as the two forces engaged each other at close range. During this critical time, other Confederates broke through the lines. "Many of the rebels being over the defenses and within less than 10 yards of my pieces," wrote Captain Andrew Cowan, whose battery was at the Copse of Trees. According to Cowan, "The infantry in front of my five pieces...turned and broke, but were rallied...by General Webb in a most gallant manner." With bravery that later earned him the Congressional Medal of Honor, Webb rallied his troops to counterstrike Armistead's men, and along with other Union regiments who arrived, they closed in on the Confederates and the combat became hand-to-hand.

The hand-to-hand fighting was brutal but brief. At the copse, Cowan fired his " last charge of canister...(a double-header) [that] literally swept the enemy from my front." Colonel Hall, whose brigade had several regiments join Webb's men in repulsing Armistead, noted that "...after a few minutes of desperate, often hand-to-hand fighting, the [Confederates]...threw down their arms and were taken prisoners of war, while the remainder broke and fled in great disorder." As "the enemy fled in disorder," described General Webb, "General Armistead was left, mortally wounded, within my lines, and 42 of the enemy who crossed the fence lay dead." Further down the line, Hancock lay wounded but he saw the supreme moment and described it superbly: "The battle-flags were ours and the victory was won."

The casualties were staggering, over 6,000 total. The charge had lasted approximately 45 minutes. General Longstreet observed that "about half of those of [Pickett's Division] who were not killed or wounded" were captured in the attack. Many units within Pickett's and Pettigrew's divisions were decimated, and the loss among officers was especially high. "Regiments that went in with colonels came out commanded by lieutenants," wrote Major John Thomas Jones of the 26th North Carolina. The carnage was most gruesome, even to the victors, as bodies lay everywhere across the mile-wide fields. "The angel of death alone can produce such a field as was presented," wrote General Hays.

DESCRIPTION OF
> OR 1: 321 (Col. Gates' Report — 20th NYS Militia / 80th NY) — Describes the "slashing area."
> OR 1: 445 & 446 (Capt. Abbott's Report — 20th MA) — Refers to "clump of trees."
> OR 1: 449 (Maj. Curtis' Report — 7th MI) — Describes Ziegler's Grove and the Copse of Trees.

The 8th Ohio Attacks the Confederate Left Flank
   OR 1: 461-462 (Col. Sawyer's Report — 8th OH)
   OR 2: 659 (Maj. Engelhard's Report — Pender's Division)
   OR 2: 666 (Gen. Lane's Brigade Report)

Fighting From Ziegler's Grove to the Angle
   OR 1: 454 (Gen. Hays' Division Report)
   OR 1: 465 (Col. Smyth's Brigade Report)
   OR 1: 467-468 (Maj. Ellis' Report** — 14th CT) — Captures 5 colors!
   OR 1: 469 (Lieut. Dent's Report — 1st DE) — Read about Lieut. William Smith.
   OR 1: 473 (Col. Bull's Report — Willard's Brigade)
   OR 1: 476 (Capt. Seeley's Report — 111th NY) — Captures 400 prisoners!
   OR 1: 477 (Lieut. Haskell's Report — 125th NY)
   OR 1: 896 (Capt. Fitzhugh's Artillery Report) — Battery K, 1st NY battery.
   OR 1: 899-900 (Lieut. Parson's Battery Report) — Battery A, 1st NJ battery.
   OR 2: 644 (Maj. Jones' Report** — Marshall's Brigade)
   OR 2: 645 (Capt. Young's Report** — 26th NC) — "It was a second Fredericksburg affair, only the wrong way."
   OR 2: 647 (Col. Shepard's Report** — Fry's Brigade) — "Every flag in the brigade excepting one was captured at or within the works of the enemy."
   OR 2: 651 (Gen. Davis' Brigade Report**) — All officers in this brigade were wounded or killed!
   OR 2: 659-660 (Maj. Engelhard's Report — Pender's Division) — General Trimble is maimed and loses a leg.
   OR 2: 666-667 (Gen. Lane's Brigade Report)
   OR 2: 671-672 (Col. Lowrance's Report** — Scales' Brigade) — Claims "the right of the brigade touched the enemy's line of breastworks" (p. 671).

The Fight at the Angle and Copse of Trees
   OR 1: 373-374, 376-377 (Gen. Hancock's II Corps Report**)
   OR 1: 417-418 (Gen. Gibbon's Division Report**)
   OR 1: 420 (Gen. Harrow's Division Report)
   OR 1: 428-429 (Gen. Webb's Brigade Report**)
   OR 1: 431 (Capt. Davis' Report — 69th PA)
   OR 1: 432 (Col. Smith's Report — 71st PA) — Captured "some 500 prisoners."
   OR 1: 433 (Col. Hesser's Report — 72nd PA) — The reports of the 69th & 71st Pennsylvania do not mention the 72nd Pennsylvania as having helped them repulse Pickett's Charge.
   OR 1: 437-441 (Col. Hall's Brigade Report**) — Read about Lieutenant Cushing.
   OR 1: 443-444 (Col. Devereux's Report — 19th MA)
   OR 1: 445-446 (Capt. Abbott's Report** — 20th MA) — Read about Lieutenant Ropes.
   OR 1: 449-450 (Maj. Curtis' Report — 7th MI)

OR 1: 451-452 (Maj. Mallon's Report — 42nd NY)
OR 1: 480 (Capt. Hazard's Artillery Report**)
OR 1: 514 (Maj. Moore's Report — 99th PA) — Cushing's battery were left with "only six men and 3 horses."
OR 1: 690 (Capt. Cowan's Battery Report**)
OR 1: 874 (Gen. Tyler's Artillery Report)
OR 1: 880 (Lieut. Weir's Battery Report)
OR 2: 386-387 (Maj. Peyton's Report** — Garnett's Brigade) — General Garnett "was shot from his horse…within about 25 paces of the stone wall."

The Fight at the "Slashing"
OR 1: 319 & 322 (Col. Gates' Report — 20th NYS Militia / 80th NY)

The Counterattack of Stannard's Brigade
OR 1: 259 (Gen. Doubleday's Division Report)
OR 1: 262 (Gen. Newton's I Corps Report)
OR 1: 349-350 (Gen. Stannard's Brigade Report)
OR 1: 352-353 (Col. Randall's Report** — 13th VT) — Hancock's wounding.
OR 1: 373, 374-375 (Gen. Hancock's II Corps Report)
OR 1: 1042 (Col. Veazey's Report** — 16th VT)
OR 2: 620 (Gen. Wilcox's Brigade Report)
OR 2: 632 (Gen. Lang's Brigade Report**)

Seeing the Charge is a Failure
OR 2: 308-309 (Gen. Lee's Report) — "More may have been required of them than they were able to perform…," wrote Lee of his retreating troops.
OR 2: 360 (Gen. Longstreet's 1st Corps Report**)
OR 2: 615 (Gen. Anderson's Division Report**)

Artillery Barrage Following the Charge
OR 1: 393 (Maj. Mulholland's Report — 116th PA) — "Perceiving the failure of their infantry to carry our position, the enemy again opened their batteries [for] another hour's fire...".
OR 1: 469 (Lieut. Dent's Report** — 1st DE) — Ordered to the Bliss ruins.
OR 1: 690 (Capt. Cowan's Report**) — His accuracy destroyed five limbers.
OR 1: 886 (Lieut. Milton's Report) — Under fire from CSA Whitworth guns.
OR 1: 896 (Capt. Fitzhugh's Artillery Report)
OR 2: 376 (Col. Cabell's Battalion Report)
OR 2: 381 (Capt. Manly's Battery Report) — Kept firing until 7:30 p.m.
OR 2: 389 (Maj. Dearing's Battalion Report) — Claims his guns repel Union advance around 6 p.m.
OR 2: 435-436 (Maj. Eshleman's Battalion Report**) — His artillery endured horrendous fire!

The Wheatfield

The Wheatfield remained a no-man's land until about 5:00 p.m. on July 3 when General Sam Crawford advanced units under Colonel William McCandless to scare out any remaining Confederates in the woods around the Wheatfield. McCandless' men charged across the Wheatfield into the Rose woods, clearing it of Confederate skirmishers. They then turned and cleared the woods behind Devil's Den. On their way toward Big Round Top, they surprised Georgia and Texas troops lying behind a stone wall. McCandless charged on their left flank and "completely rout[ed] them, taking over 200 prisoners." It was 6:00 p.m., and Union forces now had final possession of the southern part of the battlefield.

The Wheatfield was perhaps the longest contested ground at Gettysburg, having exchanged hands at least six times during the battle. The scene that evening testified to the brutal struggles for its possession. McCandless' men found thousands of rifles of all kinds strewn over the field, "the majority of which had piled on brush heaps [by the enemy, and were] ready to be burned." And "the dead of both sides lay in lines in every direction," wrote Crawford, "...together with all of our wounded, who, mingled with those of the rebels, were lying uncared for" since the previous day.

McCandless' Charge Takes the Wheatfield and Devil's Den
   OR 1: 654-656 (Gen. Crawford's Division Report**) — Recovered "upward of 7,000 stand of arms."
   OR 1: 657-658 (Col. McCandless' Brigade Report)
   OR 2: 417 (Gen. Benning's Brigade Report)
   OR 2: 423-424 (Col. DuBose's Report — 15th GA)
   OR 2: 427 (Col. Waddell's Report — 20th GA)

East Cavalry Field

The George Rummel farm was situated three miles east of Gettysburg. According to Major General Alfred Pleasonton, commander of the Union Cavalry Corps, there at "about noon the enemy threw a heavy force of cavalry against this position, with the intention of gaining our rear." A dispatch from General Howard of the 11th Corps on Cemetery Hill had earlier alerted Meade that Major General J.E.B. Stuart's Confederate cavalry were moving east. Brigadier General David Gregg was sent to stop Stuart. He had with him two brigades commanded by Colonel John McIntosh and recently-promoted Brigadier General George Armstrong Custer. Stuart had four cavalry brigades with him, and outnumbered Gregg's men. At first the fighting consisted of dismounted skirmishing and an artillery exchange. This was followed by some small mounted charges over the fields of the Rummel Farm. Then around 2:00 p.m., Stuart launched Wade Hampton's and Fitz Lee's Brigades in a full-scale mounted charge which culminated in hand-to-hand fighting when Custer and McIntosh countered the attack. In this fight, "General Hampton was severely wounded by saber cuts [to] the head" and nearly captured. The fight was a stalemate, but Union cavalry had effectively thwarted Stuart's plan to "effect a surprise on the [Union] rear." Skirmishing continued until nightfall.

CHARGES OF CUSTER AND MCINTOSH STOP J.E.B. STUART
    OR 1: 916 (Gen. Pleasonton's Cavalry Corps Report**)
    OR 1: 956-958 (Gen. Gregg's Division Report**)
    OR 1: 998-1000 (Gen. Custer's Brigade Report)
    OR 1: 1050-1051 (Col. McIntosh's Brigade Report)
    OR 2: 497 (Capt. Green's Battery Report)
    OR 2: 697-699 (Gen. Stuart's Brigade Report**)
    OR 2: 724-725 (Gen. Hampton's Brigade Report)

South Cavalry Field

Another cavalry fight occurred on the south end of the battlefield in the woods and fields immediately west of Big Round Top. This action achieved little more than the loss of a promising young cavalry officer. For several hours in the afternoon, Brigadier General Judson Kilpatrick directed two Union cavalry brigades, commanded by Brigadier Generals Wesley Merritt and Elon Farnsworth, against "the enemy's right and rear [to] annoy him." Reportedly around 5:00 p.m., Kilpatrick ordered a charge to be led by Farnsworth. The charge was made over "broken" ground against Confederate infantry of Hood's Division. Farnsworth led his forces over several stone walls and through two Confederate lines onto the Bushman and Slyder farms. The Yankee cavalrymen became surrounded, Farnsworth was killed, and the troopers had to "cut their way" out. The combat became hand-to-hand as the Union riders resorted to their sabers. In the words of one survivor, after the battle "many of our dead, together with the body of General Farnsworth, were found in the rear of the position of the enemy's second line."

THE CHARGE OF FARNSWORTH
    OR 1: 943 (Gen. Merritt's Brigade Report)
    OR 1: 993 (Gen. Kilpatrick's Division Report**) — Read about Farnsworth.

OR 1: 1005 (Col. Richmond's Brigade Report)
OR 1: 1009 (Maj. Hammond's Report — 5th NY)
OR 1: 1011-1012 (Maj. Darlington's Report — 18th PA)
OR 1: 1013 (Col. Preston's Report** — 1st VT) — Hand-to-hand fighting with sabers.
OR 1: 1018-1019 (Maj. Capehart's Report** — 1st WV) — Scaled two fences and got surrounded.
OR 2: 391-392 (Col. Scrugg's Report — 4th AL)
OR 2: 396 (Col. Sheffield's Report — 48th AL)
OR 2: 397 (Col. White's Report — 7th GA)
OR 2: 400 (Capt. Hillyer's Report** — 9th GA)
OR 2: 402-403 (Maj. McDaniel's Report** — 11th GA)

KILPATRICK'S ORDER AND FARNSWORTH'S DEATH
OR 1: 914-916 (Gen. Pleasonton's Report)
OR 1: 1005 (Col. Richmond's Brigade Report**)
OR 1: 1013 (Col. Preston's Report — 1st VT) — Farnsworth's body was found "behind the enemy's second line."

Fairfield, PA

A third cavalry engagement occurred on July 3 which ended in a total Confederate victory, but it was a small one. The 6th U.S. cavalry regiment "was ordered to proceed in the direction of Fairfield, Pa., for the purpose of intercepting a train of wagons of the enemy." About two miles from Fairfield, a brigade of Confederate cavalry stopped them just as they got "within a few hundred yards" of seizing some wagons. Opposing each other down a lane with strong fencing on either side, the Confederates made two frontal charges. The first charge was unsuccessful but the second completely routed the Union force, and the Confederates captured over 200 of them. The 7th Virginia cavalry had led the second charge, and its commanding officer reported that "Lieutenant Duncan, Company B, was conspicuous for his daring, having sabered five Yankees, running his saber entirely through one, and twisting him from his horse."

CAVALRY FIGHT BETWEEN JONES' CSA BRIGADE AND THE 6TH U.S. CAVALRY
OR 1: 948 (Lieut. Nolan's Report**) — 292 horses lost!
OR 2: 752 (Gen. Jones' Brigade Report)
OR 2: 756 (Maj. Flournoy's Report** — 6th VA) — Lt. Duncan.
OR 2: 760 (Col. Marshall's Report — 7th VA)
OR 2: 764 (Col. Lomax's Report — 11th VA)

5

Aftermath of the Battle

"The carnage....was fearful"

Over 51,000 casualties were incurred at Gettysburg, making it the bloodiest battle of the Civil War. The Union army won a decisive victory, losing just more than 23,000 in killed, wounded, missing and captured, whereas the Confederate army suffered more than 28,000 casualties. In addition, more than 5,000 horses lay dead and scattered over the battlefield. This chapter is devoted to providing the battle reports and parts of those reports that discuss the end of the Gettysburg campaign from July 4-14, 1863. Included herein are Lee's retreat from Pennsylvania, casualty reports from both armies, and the burying of the dead. Also mentioned are the honors later awarded to soldiers for exceptional deeds of valor and some of the controversies General Meade faced in the wake of his victory.

The Weather

Few reports discussed the weather for the three days of battle. The best meteorological records of Gettysburg for that time were kept by local Seminary Professor Michael Jacobs. According to his records, when Early's Division passed through Gettysburg on June 26th, it was rainy. The weather cleared the next day and remained cloudy and comfortable with highs in the 60s and low 70s through June 30th. The three days of battle remained completely cloudy, but the heat got progressively hotter. The high temperature for July 1st and for July 2nd was 76 degrees Fahrenheit. The highest temperature recorded was on July 3rd around the time of Pickett's Charge: 87 degrees — which ended up being the hottest temperature for the entire month. "During the day's fighting [July 3] the heat was very great, and the men...suffered intensely," wrote Colonel Mulholland of the 116th Pennsylvania, "[but] after sunset...the rain commenced to descend in torrents." The next day, July 4th, rain occurred in the morning and midafternoon and continued again for several days.

JULY 3, 1863 — HOT
    OR 1: 393 (Col. Mulholland's Report — 116th PA)

JULY 4-7, 1863 — RAINY
    OR 1: 801 (Col. Price's Report — 145th NY)
    OR 2: 602 (Col. Goodgame's Report — 26th NC)
    OR 2: 699 (Gen. Stuart's Division Report)

Lee's Retreat from Gettysburg

"The army will vacate its position this evening," read General Lee's orders to his Corps commanders early on July 4. Lee's army began withdrawing that night, and the last of his troops pulled out of Gettysburg in the morning of July 5. Meade ordered his 6th Corps and Union cavalry to follow and harass the Confederate army along its two retreat routes, the Fairfield Road and the Cashtown Road. The portion of the Confederate army along the Fairfield Road enroute to Hagerstown, Maryland, incurred the greatest losses as repeated Union cavalry raids captured ammunition, wagons, and especially wounded.

The Confederate wagon train of wounded alone stretched 17 miles and its "great length…made it difficult to guard," wrote Lee.

On July 6 and 7, Lee's army reached Hagerstown and he concentrated his wagon trains at Williamsport situated on the banks of the Potomac River. The Potomac was too swollen from incessant rains to allow a crossing. For several days, Union cavalry repeatedly attacked Lee's wagon train and rear guard at Williamsport, Hagerstown, Boonsborough and Funkstown but Stuart's cavalry successfully repelled them. Lee built formidable defensive works from Williamsport to Falling Waters. Meanwhile, Lee's engineers worked on building a new pontoon bridge while ferries transported wounded and prisoners across the river.

Meade arrived with the main body of the Army of the Potomac on July 12, and reconnoitered the Confederate lines the next day. By then the level of the river had dropped, the pontoon bridge was complete, and Lee began withdrawing his army across the river. Meade had prepared to attack Lee on the 14th, but by then, Lee and his men had slipped across the Potomac back to Virginia.

OVERVIEW OF LEE'S RETREAT
   OR 1: 78-92 (Gen. Meade's Dispatches**)
   OR 1: 708-709 (Gen. Howard's XI Corps Report)
   OR 2: 298-302 (Gen. Lee's Dispatches)
   OR 2: 322-323 (Gen. Lee's Report)
   OR 2: 361-362 (Gen. Longstreet's I Corps Report)
   OR 2: 448-449 (Gen. Ewell's II Corps Report)
   OR 2: 471-472 (Gen. Early's Division Report)
   OR 2: 557-559 (Gen. Rodes' Division Report**) — Claims 760 severely wounded were "left in the hands of the enemy," and many of the wounded that could walk were kept to the rear of the army only "to be captured or sacrificed in the effort to escape the enemy's cavalry."
   OR 2: 699-705 (Gen. Stuart's Division Report**)

LEE WITHDRAWS HIS ARMY
   OR 1: 523 (Col. Merrill's Report — 17th ME) — Union soldiers dig earthworks on July 4.
   OR 1: 663 (Gen. Sedgwick's VI Corps Report)
   OR 1: 957 (Gen. Gregg's Division Report) — Found many Confederate wounded abandoned around Hunterstown on July 4.
   OR 1: 666 (Gen. Wright's Division Report**) — His artillery opened on Lee's retreating forces July 5th, claiming it to be "the last firing at Gettysburg on either side."
   OR 2: 311 (Gen. Lee's General Orders No. 74**)

OR 2: 376 (Col. Cabell's Battalion Report)
OR 2: 381 (Capt. Manly's Battery Report) — Union regiments briefly engage the Confederate right on the morning of July 4.
OR 2: 389 (Maj. Dearing's Battalion Report)
OR 2: 417 (Gen. Benning's Brigade Report)
OR 2: 432-433 (Capt. Taylor's Battery Report) — leaves July 5th for Hagerstown.
OR 2: 456 (Col. Brown's Artillery Report**) — Confederate guns on the left were moved to Seminary Ridge on the 4th and placed in firing position to guard the army as it withdrew.
OR 2: 481 (Gen. Hays' Brigade Report) — Leaves July 5th for Hagerstown.
OR 2: 496 (Col. Jones' Battalion Report) — Leaves July 5th bringing up the rear of the Confederate army.
OR 2: 505 (Gen. Johnson's Division Report**) — Withdrew to Oak Ridge for July 4th "in the hope that the enemy would give us battle on ground of our own selection."
OR 2: 511 (Gen. Steuart's Brigade Report) — Entrenched on Oak Ridge, July 4.
OR 2: 534 (Col. Johnson's Report — Jones' Brigade)
OR 2: 581 (Gen. Iverson's Brigade Report)
OR 2: 593 (Col. O'Neal's Brigade Report) — Fortified Oak Ridge on July 4.
OR 2: 601 (Col. Pickens' Report — 12th AL)
OR 2: 602 (Col. Goodgame's Report — 26th AL) — Built trenches and awaited possible Union attack on July 4th before withdrawing.
OR 2: 606 (Col. Nelson's Battalion Report) — Ordered to Oak Ridge to await possible Union attack on July 4th to help cover army's retreat.
OR 2: 608 (Gen. Hill's III Corps Report)
OR 2: 615 (Gen. Anderson's Division Report)
OR 2: 625 (Gen. Wright's Brigade Report) — Left in "drenching rain."
OR 2: 645-646 (Capt. Young's Report** — 26th NC)
OR 2: 669 (Gen. Thomas' Brigade Report)
OR 2: 674 (Maj. Poague's Battalion Report)
OR 2: 699 (Gen. Stuart's Division Report) — Lee withdrew Hill's Corps first, followed by Longstreet's Corps, and then Ewell's Corps.

Union Cavalry and Infantry Harass Lee's Retreating Army
OR 1: 666-667 (Gen. Wright's Division Report)
OR 1: 679 (Gen. Neill's Brigade Report) — His brigade "picked up between 300 and 400 rebel deserters."
OR 1: 489 (Gen. French's Report** — Sickles' III Corps) — His men destroyed Lee's pontoon bridge across the Potomac at Harper's Ferry on July 5.
OR 1: 916-917 (Gen. Pleasonton's Cavalry Corps Report)
OR 1: 928-929 (Gen. Buford's Division Report**)
OR 1: 935-936 (Col. Gamble's Brigade Report**)

OR 1: 939-942 (Col. Devin's Brigade Report**)
OR 1: 943-944 (Gen. Merritt's Brigade Report)
OR 1: 948-949 (Lieut. Nolan's Report — 6th U.S.)
OR 1: 967-968 (Col. McIntosh's Brigade Report)
OR 1: 970-971 (Col. Huey's Brigade Report) — Abandoned 197 horses.
OR 1: 977-978 (Col. Gregg's Brigade Report)
OR 1: 981-982 (Maj. Avery's Report — 10th NY)
OR 1: 988-990; 993-996 (Gen. Kilpatrick's Dispatches** and Report**) — Kilpatrick exaggerates that his cavalry "destroyed the wagons of Ewell's entire corps" and took 1,500 prisoners.
OR 1: 998-1001 (Gen. Custer's Brigade Report**)
OR 1: 1006-1007 (Col. Richmond** — Farnsworth's Brigade) — Read of Lieutenant Elder's artillery at Hagerstown. "So close was the conflict, that [the] No. 1 [artillerist], turning his sponge-staff, knocked one of the enemy from his horse."
OR 1: 1009-1010 (Maj. Hammond's Report — 5th NY)
OR 1: 1011 (Maj. Darlington's Report — 18th PA)
OR 1: 1014-1016 (Col. Preston's Report — 1st VT)
OR 1: 1016-1017 (Col. Sawyer's Report** — 1st VT)
OR 1: 1019-1020 (Maj. Capehart's Report — 1st WV)
OR 1: 1032-1034 (Lieut. Calef's Battery Report**)
OR 1: 1035-1036 (Lieut. Fuller's Battery Report)
OR 2: 378 (Col. Cabell's Battalion Report)
OR 2: 418-419 (Gen. Benning's Brigade Report)
OR 2: 436-438 (Maj. Eshleman's Battalion Report)
OR 2: 488 (Col. Murchison's Report — 54th NC) — Action at Williamsport.
OR 2: 493 (Gen. Gordon's Brigade Report)
OR 2: 498-499 (Capt. Tanner's Battery Report) — Action at Williamsport.
OR 2: 576 (Capt. Hopkins** — 45th NC) — Union cavalry were disguised as Confederates!
OR 2: 581 (Gen. Iverson's Brigade Report)
OR 2: 636 (Maj. Lane's Battalion Report)
OR 2: 654-655 (Maj. Richardson's Report** — Garnett's Battalion) — Discusses General Imboden's protection of the Confederate wagon train.
OR 2: 752- 754 (Gen. Jones' Brigade Report) — Two brothers who fall in battle.
OR 2: 760-762 (Col. Marshall's Report — 7th VA)
OR 2: 764-765 (Col. Lomax's Report — 11th VA)

CONFEDERATES WAIT AT HAGERSTOWN FOR MEADE TO ATTACK, JULY 7-12
OR 2: 353 (Gen. Pendleton's Artillery Report)
OR 2: 389-390 (Maj. Dearing's Battalion Report)
OR 2: 432-433 (Capt. Taylor's Battery Report)

OR 2: 534 (Col. Johnson's Report — Jones' Brigade)
OR 2: 606 (Capt. Nelson's Battalion Report)
OR 2: 609 (Gen. Hill's III Corps Report)
OR 2: 615 (Gen. Anderson's Division Report)
OR 2: 644 (Maj. Jones' Report — 26th NC)
OR 2: 672 (Col. Lowrance's Report — 34th NC)

CONFEDERATES RECROSS THE POTOMAC RIVER INTO VIRGINIA, JULY 13-14
OR 1: 942 (Col. Devin's Brigade Report)
OR 1: 990 (Gen. Kilpatrick's Division Report**)
OR 1: 999 & 1001 (Gen. Custer's Brigade Report)
OR 1: 1034 (Lieut. Calef's Battery Report**)
OR 2: 353 (Gen. Pendleton's Artillery Report)
OR 2: 370 (Gen. Kershaw's Brigade Report)
OR 2: 377 (Col. Cabell's Battalion Report)
OR 2: 390 (Maj. Dearing's Battalion Report)
OR 2: 430 (Col. Alexander's Artillery Report)
OR 2: 433 (Capt. Taylor's Battery Report)
OR 2: 493 (Gen. Gordon's Brigade Report)
OR 2: 505 (Gen. Johnson's Division Report)
OR 2: 603 (Col. Carter's Battalion Report) — Carter's batteries covered the army's crossing at Falling Waters.
OR 2: 606 (Col. Nelson's Battalion Report)
OR 2: 609 (Gen. Hill's III Corps Report) — General Pettigrew is killed.
OR 2: 615 (Gen. Anderson's Division Report)
OR 2: 639-642 (Gen. Heth's Division Report**) — General Pettigrew's death.
OR 2: 644 (Maj. Jones' Report — 26th NC) — General Pettigrew's death.
OR 2: 648 (Col. Shepard's Report** — 7th TN)
OR 2: 653 (Col. Garnett's Battalion**) — Fought with Custer's cavalry at Falling Waters and protected the Confederate pontoon bridge.
OR 2: 664 (Col. Perrin's Brigade Report)
OR 2: 667 (Gen. Lane's Brigade Report**)
OR 2: 672 (Col. Lowrance's Report — 34th NC)
OR 2: 676 (Maj. McIntosh's Battalion Report)

Losses Reported by the Armies

In the aftermath of Gettysburg, more than 7,000 soldiers lay dead on the battlefield. The most comprehensive casualty returns for both armies are referenced below and give losses for each regiment, brigade, division and corps. In terms of the total losses given, the Union army reported 3,155 killed, 14,529 wounded, and 5,365 captured or missing, for an aggregate of 23,049 casualties. The Confederate army reported 2,592 killed,

12,709 wounded, and 5,150 captured or missing, for an aggregate of 20,451 casualties. The Confederate casualty totals reported are generally regarded to be low by nearly 8,000. Furthermore, both armies' casualty returns are low or misleading regarding the number killed because they do not factor in the number who died of their wounds shortly after the battle and the number of missing who were later found dead. Today, Gettysburg National Military Park officially acknowledges that precise casualty numbers "will never be known," but "the best estimate of those killed and mortally wounded in the Battle of Gettysburg numbered well over 10,000" (www.nps.gov/gett/getttour).

Futhermore, there are other numerous casualty lists throughout the *Official Records* given by individual regiments, brigades, divisions and corps of both armies, but beware of discrepancies here too. As an example, the losses reported by the 5th and 6th New Jersey regiments (see OR 1: 576 & 578) do not agree entirely with their losses as recorded in their brigade commander's report (see OR 1: 571). This is common. Similar discrepancies in tallying exist for casualty reports given at all levels of command for both armies. The preface printed with the Confederate casualty returns states it best: "In computing the 'grand total,' the figures supplied by brigade, division, and corps commanders have generally been adopted; but, whether taken in detail or as a whole, the compilation can only be regarded as approximative [sic]."

Union regiments spent July 4, 5, and 6 burying their dead in shallow graves. After the army moved out in pursuit of Lee, many bodies still remained to be buried, particularly Union dead on the first day's fields, and Confederate dead on the south end of the battlefield. In addition, about 5,000 horses lay dead on the ground as well. No cumulative totals of horse casualties are found in the *Official Records*, but commanders of batteries and cavalry regiments from both armies frequently mentioned horse losses in their reports. Horses were struck and hurt unmercifully during the battle. Killing horses disabled cannon and riders, which made the animals prime targets. Some were especially vivid in describing the vulnerability of horses at the front. Union Lieutenant Colonel Freeman McGilvery reported that during the engagement at the Peach Orchard on July 2, "my horse was hit four times in the foreshoulder and breast by musketry, once on the fore-leg by shell, and once on the hip by spent solid shot, of which wounds he soon after died."

Casualty Returns & Care of the Wounded
OR 1: 24-25 (Medical Inspector Cuyler's Report**)

OR 1: 25-28 (Medical Inspector Vollum's Report**) — "The period of ten days following the battle of Gettysburg was the occasion of the greatest amount of human suffering know to this nation..."
OR 1: 173-192 (Union Army Casualty Returns)
OR 1: 195-199 (Medical Director Letterman's Report**)
OR 2: 326-328 (Medical Director Guild's Report**)
OR 2: 329-346 (Confederate Army Casualty Returns)

Burying the Dead and Gathering Arms from the Field
OR 1: 119-120 (Gen. Meade's Dispatches to Gen. Halleck**) — The burial of Confederate dead by the Union army.
OR 1: 422 (Gen. Harrow's Division Report)
OR 1: 428 (Gen. Webb's Brigade Report)
OR 1: 432 (Capt. Davis' Report — 69th PA)
OR 1: 450 (Maj. Curtis' Report — 7th MI)
OR 1: 452 (Col. Mallon's Report — 7th MI)
OR 1: 454 (Gen. Hays' Division Report)
OR 1: 465 (Col. Smyth's Brigade Report)
OR 1: 470 (Maj. Hill's Report — 12th NJ)
OR 1: 491-492 (Gen. French's Report — Sickles' III Corps)
OR 1: 503 (Capt. Bowen's Report — 114th PA)
OR 1: 512 (Col. Higgins' Report — 86th NY)
OR 1: 559 (Col. Brewster's Report — Excelsior Brigade)
OR 1: 596-597 (Gen. Sykes' V Corps Report**) — See table on dead and arms.
OR 1: 604 (Gen. Barnes' Division Report)
OR 1: 618 (Col. Rice's Report — Vincent's Brigade)
OR 1: 626 (Col. Chamberlain's Report** — 20th ME) — Buried the dead by "marking each grave by a headboard made of ammunition boxes."
OR 1: 655-656 (Gen. Crawford's Division Report**)
OR 1: 658 (Col. McCandless' Brigade Report**)
OR 1: 659 (Col. Fisher's Brigade Report)
OR 1: 776 (Gen. Williams' Division Report)
OR 1: 786 (Col. McDougall's Brigade Report)
OR 1: 794 (Col. Wooster's Report — 20th CT)
OR 1: 795 (Col. Sudsburg's Report — 3rd MD)
OR 1: 831 (Gen. Geary's Division Report**) — Many firearms were carried away by local citizens.
OR 1: 837 (Col. Candy's Brigade Report) — Only a "few of the enemy's dead were buried" because the army had to leave.
OR 1: 850 (Col. Cobham's Report — Kane's Brigade)
OR 1: 858 (Gen. Greene's Brigade Report)

Artillery Lost and Captured
- OR 1: 357 (Col. Wainwright's Artillery Report) — Wilber's Battery lost one gun near the Seminary on July 1.
- OR 1: 583 (Capt. Randolph's Artillery Report) — Smith's Battery lost three guns at Devil's Den on July 2.
- OR 1: 755 (Capt. Heckman's Battery Report) — Heckman's Battery lost two guns in town on July 1.
- OR 1: 882 (Col. McGilvery's Artillery Report) — Thompson's Battery lost one gun near the Peach Orchard on July 2.
- OR 1: 890 (Capt. Thompson's Battery Report**)
- OR 2: 357 (Col. Baldwin's Ordnance Report) — Lee's army captured seven Union guns and lost zero in the battle.

Examples of Horse Losses & Sufferings
- OR 1: 465 (Col. Smyth's Brigade Report**)
- OR 1: 592 (Lieut. James' Battery Report) — Had to destroy 16 horses "owing to ... their severe wounds."
- OR 1: 751 (Major Osborn's Artillery Report**) — The only report giving a tabular listing of "horses killed" by unit.
- OR 1: 882-883 (Col. McGilvery's Artillery Report**) — Captains Thompson and Bigelow lost all of their horses used in retreating from the Peach Orchard.
- OR 2: 355-356 (Gen. Pendleton's Artillery Report**) — Read "remarks" in table.
- OR 2: 378 (Col. Cabell's Battalion Report**) — Table gives horse losses per battery.
- OR 2: 611-612 (Col. Walker's Artillery Report**) — The lack of horseshoes accounts for many horse losses on the march to Gettysburg.
- OR 2: 635-636 (Maj. Lane's Battalion Report)
- OR 2: 653 (Col. Garnett's Battalion Report**) — Lack of forage for horses.
- OR 2: 676 (Maj. McIntosh's Battalion Report) — No corn for horses.
- OR 2: 709 (Gen. Stuart's Division Report)

Honors for Deeds of Valor

The U.S. Congress awarded 63 Medals of Honor to Union soldiers for their deeds of valor at Gettysburg. However, only 21 of them are mentioned in the *Official Records* because they were the total number of recipients at the time of the publication in 1889. Most of the other recipients received their Medals of Honor in the 1890s, including Joshua Chamberlain (1893) and Daniel Sickles (1897).

The Confederate Government desired to award similar medals for exceptional courage and bravery on the field of battle, but delays in production compelled the government to publish a "Roll of Honor" series with recipients names until such medals could be furnished. In the *Official Records*, only two "Roll of Honor" lists for the Battle of Gettysburg are included showing a total of 42 recipients from just six regimental units.

In January of 1864, Congresses of both sides issued resolutions thanking the officers and men of their respective armies.

MEDAL OF HONOR AND CONFEDERATE ROLL OF HONOR
OR 2: 282 (Union) — Incomplete (only 21 recipients listed).
OR 2: 774-776 (Confederate) – Incomplete, only six regiments listed.

CONGRESSIONAL RESOLUTIONS OF THANKS
OR 1: 140 (Union) — Specifically mentions Generals Hooker, Meade, and Howard in repelling Lee's army.
OR 2: 326 (Confederacy) — Specifically thanks Lee's army for victories over the preceding two years

Meade's Controversies

After Gettysburg, Lee and Meade both offered their resignations to their respective Presidents. Both were declined. Lee offered to resign because he had lost. Meade offered to resign because of Lincoln's frustrations over him for not having crushed Lee's army during its retreat. But the controversy with Lincoln was just one of several that Meade had to contend with in the aftermath of Gettysburg. Most were the result of conflict with generals among his high command. Major General Daniel Butterfield, his Chief of Staff, was jealous of Meade and resented him deeply. Meade disliked Butterfield, too, but Butterfield had been Hooker's Chief of Staff and there had been no time to replace him until after Gettysburg, which he promptly did (by appointing Brigadier General Andrew Humphreys in his place). Major General Abner Doubleday, who commanded the 1st Corps at Gettysburg on July 1, resented Meade for having replaced him the next day, and worse yet, with a junior officer (Major General John Newton). Instead of accepting his old divisional command, he resigned his position immediately after the battle.

But there are two other controversies Meade faced for which there is correspondence in the *Official Records*. First, his official report when first issued and circulated was hotly received by Major General Henry Slocum, commander of the 12th Corps, and Brigadier General John Robinson of the 1st Corps. Both were intensely angered with Meade's report for not adequately recognizing the brave services of their men in the battle, and both wrote Meade letters pointing out the errors and injustices of his report. Meade eventually made substantial corrections in response to Slocum's criticisms. Second, Major General Dan Sickles resented Meade for criticizing his actions on July 2 as having contributed to the destruction of his 3rd Corps. Although Meade's official report was gentle with Sickles, Meade's boss, General-in-Chief Henry Halleck reported to the War Department that Sickles' advance was an "error which nearly proved fatal in the battle" (OR 1: 16). Deeply paranoid of receiving any blame, he sought to discredit Meade's conduct at Gettysburg in an attempt to avert any dishonor. A letter designed to that effect was written under the name "Historicus" (most likely Sickles) and published in the *New York Herald* in March of 1864. It appeared just after a Congressional committee had begun investigating Meade's conduct at Gettysburg. One of the centerpieces to the investigation was determining whether or not Meade wanted to retreat from Gettysburg on the night he held his council of war at the Leister farmhouse on July 2. Accusations that he did threatened his rightful credit to victory. Key witnesses in the hearings who testified against Meade included Generals Sickles, Butterfield, and Doubleday.

Ironically, Congress had issued their resolution of thanks, conspicuously recognizing General Meade, just weeks before the official investigation into Meade's conduct got underway. Fortunately, Meade was exonerated one year later, but the ordeal forever soured his victory at Gettysburg.

CONTROVERSY WITH LINCOLN
   OR 1: 700 (Gen. Howard's Letter to Pres. Lincoln)

CONTROVERSY OVER MEADE'S OFFICIAL REPORT
   OR 1: 120-121 (Gen. Meade's corrections to his Official Report)
   OR 1: 291 (Gen. Robinson's letter of frustration to Gen. Meade**)
   OR 1: 763-770 (Gen. Slocum's Correspondence with Meade**)

MEADE-SICKLES CONTROVERSY
   OR 1: 16 (Gen. Halleck's Report**)
   OR 1: 70-71 (Gen. Meade's Dispatch) — Meade considers Pipe Creek on July 1 prior to reaching Gettysburg.
   OR 1: 116 (Gen. Meade's Report)
   OR 1: 121-139 (Gen. Meade's Report**) — Read "Historicus."

MINUTES AND LETTERS REGARDING THE COUNCIL OF WAR
   OR 1: 73-74, 124-127, 139 (Gen. Meade's correspondence)

6

Miscellaneous Incidents & Events

"...and there ended the Pennsylvania Campaign"

John Burns was a citizen of Gettysburg who volunteered to fight for the Union army during the battle. His patriotism made for one of the most storied incidents after the battle, and even compelled President Lincoln to meet and honor the local town hero. This chapter is devoted to the dozens of other equally fascinating (but lesser known) stories and incidents as reported in the *Official Records*. Included herein are parts of battle reports detailing stories of lack of shoes, death by friendly-fire, disputes over honor, cowardice, inspiration, competition, and heroics.

JOHN BURNS AND THE 150TH PENNSYLVANIA REGIMENT
    OR 1: 255 (Gen. Doubleday's First Corps Report)
THE KILLING OF "JENNIE" WADE
    OR 1: 741 (Capt. Koenig's Report — 58th NY)
COLONEL MORROW'S CONVERSATIONS WITH THE REBELS WHILE A PRISONER
    OR 1: 272-273 (Col. Morrow's Report — 24th MI)
ARMY POLITICS — HANCOCK'S REVISED REPORT
    OR 1: 377 (Gen. Hancock's Addenda)

Difficulties (including Shoes!)

Marching was the greatest difficulty most often mentioned in reports besides combat. When the battle started, for example, both armies were stretched out and fragmented over 20 miles along more than a dozen roads in many directions, so fatigue, fainting, and heat exhaustion were commonly reported by officers rushing their troops to Gettysburg as fast as possible. Union Major General John Sedgwick's 6th Corps receives the distinction for having traveled the farthest, reaching Gettysburg "on the afternoon of July 2, after a march of more than 30 miles." When Sedgwick's lead units reached Little Round Top in time to help repel Longstreet's assault, the Confederates they engaged were as worn out as they were. Longstreet had spent the day marching and countermarching his troops so much that an officer of the 4th Alabama claimed his men had marched "without interruption 24 miles to reach the battlefield" on Seminary Ridge. And after getting into position, Longstreet immediately ordered his men to attack whereupon the first units subsequently "advanced at a double-quick step fully one mile to engage the enemy" at Devil's Den and Little Round Top. It was amazing that they could even fight. In fact, reports from the first two days of battle reveal most soldiers were similarly exhausted when forced into combat.

Also, both armies lacked shoes, and complaints of such were most prevalent in Union reports! Beginning in the 1870s, Confederate General Henry Heth began widely publicizing a story that the battle occurred accidentally because his Confederates came to Gettysburg in search of shoes. He had even written his report to substantiate this claim (see OR 2: 637). The story's popularity peaked in the 1960s when Heth's memoirs were republished, and it still persists, but it has no basis. As Union General Slocum stated in his report, "...many of [my] men were destitute of shoes" too. Moreover, Confederates had gathered shoes and supplies from other towns. Confederate General Jubal Early had already secured 1200 pairs of shoes from York, as well as money, hats, and socks, prior to the battle, and had already searched Gettysburg for supplies (including shoes) on June 26 — four days prior to Heth's arrival in Gettysburg, and certainly Heth was aware of Early's raid. In the years after the battle, Heth told his story to avoid being blamed for starting Lee's worst loss, but the *Official Records* clearly expose Heth's shoe excuse as a myth.

Exhaustion from Long Marches, No Shoes, Lack of Meals, and Heat Stroke

OR 1: 348 (Gen. Stannard's Brigade Report) — Averaged 18 miles per day.
OR 1: 435 (Col. Hall's Brigade Report)
OR 1: 523 (Col. Merrill's Report — 17th ME) — "Many of the men were without shoes."
OR 1: 551 (Capt. Donovan's Report — 16th MA)
OR 1: 568 (Capt. Lockwood's Report — 120th NY)
OR 1: 573-574 (Col. Bailey's Report** — 2nd NH)
OR 1: 597 (Capt. Bates' Ambulance Report) — Condition of horses.
OR 1: 606 (Lt. Ayer's Ambulance Report) — Condition of horses.
OR 1: 663 (Gen. Sedgwick's Sixth Corps Report) — Marched over 30 miles to reach Gettysburg on July 2.
OR 1: 665 (Gen. Wright's Brigade Report)
OR 1: 723 (Col. Smyth's Brigade Report) — Many lacked shoes.
OR 1: 761 (Gen. Slocum's XII Corps Report) — Complained of lack of shoes.
OR 2: 354 (Gen. Pendleton's Artillery Report)
OR 2: 394 (Col. Perry's Report — 4th AL) — Marched "24 miles to reach the battle-field" on July 2.
OR 2: 590 (Maj. Lambeth's Report — 14th NC)
OR 2: 596 (Col. Hall's Report** — 5th AL) — Men fainted from exhaustion.
OR 2: 611 (Col. Walker's Artillery Report**) — Lack of horseshoes.
OR 2: 619 (Gen. Wilcox's Brigade Report) — His men "had nothing to eat."
OR 2: 653-654 (Col. Garnett's Battalion Report) — Condition of horses.

Removing Fences for Earthworks and to Clear Obstacles

OR 1: 532 (Gen. Humphreys' Division Report)
OR 1: 556 (Maj. Bodine's Report — 26th PA)
OR 1: 745 (Major Ledig's Report — 75th PA)

Construction of Breastworks and Rifle Pits
OR 1: 812 (Col. Colgrove's Report)
OR 1: 823 & 824 (Col. Hawley's Report)
OR 1: 854 (Col. Walker's Report)

Detailed to Watch Prisoners
OR 1: 471 (Maj. Hopper's Report — 10th NY)

Dangers

Officers sometimes described dangers other than engaging the enemy, several of which are listed below, but the most shocking were instances when their troops suffered casualties unintentionally at the hands of their own army. The most common occurrences of such "friendly-fire" happened when cannon supported infantry engagements. A good example is the 15th Massachusetts who left their position near the Angle on Cemetery Ridge and advanced to the Emmitsburg Road near the Codori farm in the evening of July 2 prior to the Confederate attack against Cemetery Ridge. "Upon the approach of the enemy," wrote their colonel, "batteries in our rear opened fire with grape and canister, by which we lost a large number of killed and wounded."

Interestingly, the most reports of losses from artillery friendly-fire came from Union troops fighting in the early morning hours on Culp's Hill. It was there that the lines of the armies were the closest of anywhere on the field for the longest duration, and Union artillery fired over the Federal line inflicted Union casualties when either shots fell short, exploded prematurely, or when Union infantry counterattacked. At least four Federal regiments suffered losses this way. In the case of the 20th Connecticut, who repulsed several Confederate advances in the woods around Pardee Field, their commanding officer claimed, "At times it became necessary...to retire my whole command to save it from being destroyed by our own artillery."

Friendly Fire
OR 1: 319 (Col. Gates' Report — 20th NYS Militia / 80th NY) — Confederate batteries supporting Pickett's Charge did "as much damage in their own ranks as in ours."
OR 1: 423 (Col. Joslin's Report — 15th MA)
OR 1: 781 (Gen. Ruger's Report — Williams' Division)
OR 1: 784-785 (Col. McDougall's Brigade Report**)
OR 1: 793-794 (Col. Wooster's Report — 20th CT)
OR 1: 801 (Col. Price's Report** — 145th NY)

OR 1: 803 (Col. Selfridge's Report** — 46th PA)
OR 1: 829 (Gen. Geary's Division Report) — Troops of the 66th Ohio on Culp's Hill "advanced too far, and fell by our own artillery fire."
OR 1: 862 (Col. Redington's Report — 60th NY) — Killed some of their own skirmishers in the darkness of July 2 on Culp's Hill.
OR 1: 939 (Col. Devin's Brigade Report)
OR 2: 583 (Gen. Doles' Brigade Report**) — He lost men on both July 1st and 3rd to Confederate guns.

Casualties from Short Fuses and Defective Shells
OR 1: 724 (Col. Smith's Brigade Report)
OR 2: 456 (Col. Brown's Artillery Report)
OR 2: 588 (Gen. Ramseur's Brigade Report)

Officers and Men Risking Their Lives to Inspire the Troops
OR 1: 450 (Maj. Curtis' Report — 7th MI) — Read about Colonel Steele.
OR 1: 466 (Col. Smyth's Brigade Report) — Read about Lt. Colonel Pierce.
OR 2: 619 (Gen. Wilcox's Brigade Report) — Wounded regimental commanders.
OR 2: 663 (Col. Perrin's Brigade Report) — Read about Captain Haskell.

Retrieving the Wounded
OR 1: 455 (Gen. Hays' Division Report) — Read about Lieutenant Sullivan.
OR 1: 469 (Lieut. Dent's Report — 1st DE)
OR 1: 597-598 (Capt. Bates' Ambulance Report**)
OR 2: 414 (Gen. Benning's Brigade Report)

Disputes & Discrepancies

Enemy colors were the most sought-after prizes in combat. But in the aftermath of Pickett's Charge, several Union officers disputed how various Confederate flags were captured. "Two battle-flags of the enemy were taken by men of my regiment, but were torn from the lances by men of other regiments," wrote Union Colonel Heath of the 19th Maine. Union Major Sylvanus Curtis of the 7th Michigan reported witnessing even worse "dastardly conduct" toward Private William Demming of his regiment who "had shot a rebel color-bearer and taken the color from him." While Demming reloaded his gun "with the flag by his side," wrote Curtis, "a [Union] colonel rode up to him and, menacing him with his saber, forced the color from him; even threatening to cut him down if he did not give it up." Unfortunately, Curtis was never able to identify the officer.

Other disputes arose among fellow officers and units over who deserved credit for key actions, especially when top generals failed to remember. When Union General Hancock issued a circular several days after the battle calling for the identity of "a certain regiment" that he wished to recognize for having "charged a rebel regiment" on July 2 at his order, regimental commanders of Willard's Brigade vied for the honor. They even disagreed over what happened, especially over who recaptured some Union guns, and how many, during their charge against Barksdale's Confederates that afternoon. "I am unable to settle the conflict...," wrote their brigade commander, Lieutenant Colonel James Bull, in his report issued one month after Gettysburg.

The most fascinating dispute occurred between Generals Lee and Meade over Lee's retreat. "I have seen in the Northern papers what purported to be an official dispatch of General Meade," wrote Lee in a dispatch dated July 21. Meade had written of General Kilpatrick's cavalry who had "captured 2 guns, 3 battle-flags, and upward of 1,500 prisoners" from the Confederate army as it retired across the Potomac River at Falling Waters on July 14. "This dispatch has been copied into the Richmond papers," Lee further stated, "and...I desire to state that it is incorrect." Lee claimed the guns had been abandoned, suggested the flags were similarly left behind by stragglers, and that "no prisoners were taken by the enemy in battle." Meade submitted a thorough rebuttal, based on Kilpatrick's official report, in the hopes "that justice may be done...and the truth of history vindicated." But Confederate General Henry Heth, whose men were the ones attacked by Kilpatrick's cavalry, angrily asserted that Kilpatrick had lied to Meade. In his report given in September, Heth stated, "[Kilpatrick] knows full well that no organized body of men was captured; not even a company...General Kilpatrick, in order to glorify himself, has told a deliberate falsehood."

Lastly, time deserves mention. Time is the most frequent discrepancy found in officer reports because standardized time did not exist until time zones were established by the leading railroads in 1883. No better example of this problem is the variety of times given for the cannonade preceding Pickett's Charge (see below). And worse, since reports were written after the battle, officers occasionally confused the timing of events. For example, Major Willis of the 119th New York reported that it was on July 2 that "about 4 p.m. opened was is said to be the grandest cannonade of the war, which lasted for about five hours." That cannonade did not occur until the next day, and it lasted only two hours! Of course, this much discrepancy was rare, and most times given in reports for any event ranged about one-to-two hours.

COMPETITION AND DISPUTES OVER CAPTURING THE ENEMY'S COLORS
OR 1: 319 (Col. Gates' Report — 80th NY)
OR 1: 422 (Col. Heath's Report** — 19th ME)

OR 1: 450 (Maj. Curtis' Report** — 7th MI) — Read about Private Deming.

DISPUTES OVER HOW TO REPORT BATTLE
OR 1: 474 (Col. Bull's Report — Willard's Brigade)
OR 1: 474-475 (Col. MacDougall's Report — 111th NY) — See General Hancock's circular.
OR 1: 681 (Gen. Shaler's Brigade Report) — Shaler's disputes General Meade's report for having acknowledged the wrong brigade.
OR 1: 682 (Gen. Meade's Letter) — Meade corrects his report for Shaler.
OR 1: 989-991 (Gen. Kilpatrick's Report**) — Dispatches from Lee and Meade over Kilpatrick.
OR 2: 641-642 (Gen. Heth's Report**).

DISCREPANCIES IN REPORTED TIMES FOR THE CANNONADE OF JULY 3.
OR 1: 382 (Col. McKeen's Report — Cross' Brigade) — Began at 4 p.m.
OR 1: 383 (Maj. Cross' Report — 5th NH) — Began at 2 p.m.
OR 1: 391 (Capt. Burke's Report — 88th NY) — Began at 10 a.m.
OR 1: 423 (Col. Joslin's Report — 15th MA) — Began at 1 p.m.
OR 1: 743 (Maj. Willis' Report — 119th NY) — Claims this cannonade began the previous day!

Dishonor & Defeat

The single largest instance of cowardice reported happened on July 3. According to Union Major Charles Ewing of the 4th New Jersey, over 400 Union troops fled Cemetery Ridge "about noon...at the time of the enemy's terrific attack upon the left center." The time and description suggests the fugitives fled either during the cannonade or Pickett's Charge that afternoon, or both. Ewing's regiment was "in charge of the [Federal] ammunition train of the Artillery Reserve" on the Baltimore Pike when they saw the fugitives coming their way. "I immediately deployed [west] across the road in the woods," wrote Ewing, whereupon his men stopped "between 400 and 500" fleeing Federals at bayonet point.

While several other instances of cowardice were reported, evidence of other dishonorable actions is revealed by what is missing from reports. Officers of regiments defeated in battle, forced to retreat, or through whom the enemy had broken and pierced the line, often did not report their failure. This is most glaringly evident in the reports by Confederates Colonel E. P. Alexander and General Jubal Early, which make no mention of Lee's attack and defeat of July 3. Interestingly, their writings in the postwar years would heavily focus on explaining the actions of their army in defense of Confederate honor.

Instances of Cowardice & A.W.O.L.
OR 1: 284 (Gen. Culter's Brigade Report**) — "Captain Kellogg...deserves special notice...for having cut down with his saber a cowardly field officer."

OR 1: 389 (Lieut. Smith's Report — 69th NY) — Lieutenant Neill is charged with being absent without leave from July 2-4.

OR 1: 444 (Col. Devereaux's Report — 19th MA)

OR 1: 794 (Col. Wooster's Report — 20th CT)

OR 1: 902 (Major Ewing's Report — 4th NJ**)

OR 2: 395 (Maj. Campbell's Report — 47th AL) — The "colonel remained so far behind" the lines.

OR 2: 410 (Col. Work's Report — 1st TX) — Singles out privates Childer and Brooks.

OR 2: 533 (Col. Dungan's Report — 48th VA) — "I am glad to report that no individual cases of cowardice have yet been reported to me."

Confederate Reports that Ignore Or Hardly Mention Day Three
OR 2: 430 (Col. E. P. Alexander's Battalion Report)

OR 2: 471 (Gen. Early's Division Report)

Arrests for Disobedience or Misconduct
OR 1: 469 (Lt. Dent's Report — 1st DE) — General Hancock arrested Lieutenant Colonel Harris on July 2 for withdrawing his skirmish line from the Bliss farm without orders.

7

Interesting Quotes From the Soldiers

"... it is a mystery to me that they were not all hit ...."

The battle had been so horrendous, it is a wonder that anyone survived. But thousands did, and at the 75th Anniversary Reunion of Blue and Gray at Gettysburg in 1938, many gathered for what would be their last meeting. In the spirit of reconciliation, former enemies shook hands, shared meals, and swapped lots of fascinating stories and tales of their exploits in the battle. But over the years, nostalgia, embellishment, and forgetfulness had fogged many a memory. This chapter is devoted to listing some of the interesting quotes and anecdotes from battle reports that reveal the most expressive and prominent combat experiences as remembered by the soldiers while the battle still remained crisp in their minds.

The quotes herein are presented with the soldier's name and unit, and are grouped by the day of battle for which the quote was given. Some require a greater explanation of the circumstances in which they were made or of the events they refer to in the battle, while other quotes stand alone. The latter has been done with those quotes that either express an experience fairly common to many soldiers, or are of an exceptionally profound nature for which any explanation would only detract from their effect. Of course, citations are provided after every quote should the reader wish to investigate them further.

Union Army of the Potomac

July 1

"Lieutenant Roder now fired the first gun (which opened the sanguinary battle of Gettysburg)..." – Lieutenant Calef, Calef's Battery, in his official report as printed in 1889. The original report was written July 27, 1863, however the words in parentheses were probably added years later as Calef revised his report to clearly claim for his unit the honor of opening the battle (OR 1: 1031).

"All of the color guard were killed or wounded" – Col. Morrow, 24th MI (OR 1: 270).

"[We] captured more prisoners than the regiment numbered" – Col. MacThomson, 107th PA (OR 1: 304).

"... [my] horse was shot under [me] five times during this brief contest" – Colonel Gates, 80th New York, regarding the last stand made by his troops at the Seminary before retreating through town (OR 1: 321).

"My loss in killed and wounded was two-thirds of my officers and half of my men" – Colonel Gates, 80th New York (OR 1: 322).

"I saved the regiment and lost the colors" – Colonel Dwight, 149th PA (OR 1: 342).

"I believe our brigade was the last to leave the field" – Captain Irvin, 149th PA, claiming honor for Stone's brigade in the retreat from Seminary Ridge (OR 1: 345).

"The regiment numbered ... before the battle nearly 400 at roll-call; [however] in the evening [of July 1] but 2 officers ... and 84 men were present" – Colonel Huidekoper, 150th PA (OR 1: 347).

"As the last piece of battery was coming away, all its horses were shot..." – Captain Hall, 2nd Maine Battery (OR 1: 359).

"...reached Gettysburg ... over the road, rendered almost impassable by mud" – General Birney, Birney's Division, describing the difficulty of the Emmitsburg road because of the previous "passage over it of the First and Eleventh Corps through the rain" (OR 1: 482).

"These hills I regarded as of the utmost importance, since their possession by the enemy would give him an opportunity of enfilading our entire left wing and center with a fire which could not fail to dislodge us from our position" – General Geary regarding Big and Little Round Top which his troops initially occupied on July 1 (OR 1: 825).

"...the cemetery commanded every eminence within easy range ... [from which the enemy] could be completely swept by artillery" – General Howard describing the importance of Cemetery Hill (OR 1: 702).

"Cemetery Hill is the commanding point of the whole position..." – General von Steinwehr, whose division occupied the hill from July 1 to 3 (OR 1: 721).

The battle today "has mortified me and will disgrace me. Please inform me frankly if you disapprove of my conduct to-day, that I may know what to do" – General Howard, XI Corps, to General Meade on the evening of July 1 regarding the retreat of the Federal army that day while under his command (OR 1: 696).

July 2

"...the enemy were now coming up in columns en masse, while we had but a single line of battle to receive the shock" – General Ward, Ward's Brigade, depicting Longstreet's attack on his men at Devil's Den (OR 1: 493).

"The conduct of my command was admirable. They were all in exposed positions...", Captain Randolph, Randolph's Artillery Brigade, whose batteries were at the Devil's Den, Wheatfield, and Peach Orchard (OR 1: 585).

"...the key of the battle-field was entrusted to my keeping..." – General Sykes, V Corps, writing of being ordered to defend Little Round Top (OR 1: 592).

"An officer fired his pistol at my head with one hand, while he handed me his sword with the other" – Colonel Chamberlain, 20th Maine (OR 1: 624).

"...their heroic conduct alone saved the command at least, if not the entire left of the army, from disaster ..." – General Barnes, Barnes' Division, in praise of Vincent's Brigade defending Little Round Top (OR 1: 602).

"The carnage ... was fearful" – Captain Woolsey, 5th New Jersey, of the fight at the Peach Orchard (OR 1: 576).

"Mentioning the names of a few would be doing an injustice to the rest" – Colonel Kelly, Kelly's Brigade, praising the officers and men who fought in the Wheatfield (OR 1: 386).

"...in a few minutes we lost nearly half of the regiment" – Major Floyd-Jones, 11th U.S., describing how quickly his regulars were overwhelmed by the final Confederate attack in the Wheatfield on July 2 (OR 1: 650).

"I took ... the largest proportionate loss in the corps in that fight, and, I think, in the army, in this or any other battle" – Colonel Madill, 141st Pennsylvania, referring to his regiment after fighting at the Peach Orchard (OR 1: 505).

"I was obliged to leave my dead and seriously wounded on the field..." – Colonel Lakeman, 3rd Maine, describing the overwhelming Confederate attack on the Peach Orchard (OR 1: 507).

"... my horse was hit four times in the fore-shoulder and breast by musketry, once on the fore-leg by shell, and once on the hip by spent solid shot, of which wounds he soon after died" – Colonel McGilvery, Peach Orchard (OR 1: 883).

"...it is a mystery to me that they were not all hit by the enemy's fire, as they were surrounded and fired upon from almost every direction" – Colonel McGilvery remarking how six of his men hauled off a cannon by hand and narrowly escape Confederates who had shot down every horse in their limbers at the Trostle Farm (OR 1: 882).

"...having marched 34 miles within seventeen hours," the three regiments "had barely gotten into position" when Confederates drove retreating Union soldiers back through their lines. Quickly, they "delivered two volleys into the ranks of the advancing rebels, and immediately after charged their column..." – Colonel Nevin, Nevin's Brigade, on joining the Pennsylvania Reserves under General Crawford in driving the Confederates back across the Wheatfield (OR 1: 684-685).

"...although we inflicted severe punishment upon the enemy, and stopped his advance, we there lost in killed and wounded more than two-thirds of our men and officers who were engaged" – Captain Coates, 1st Minnesota, regarding the regiment's charge to the Codori-Trostle thicket (OR 1: 425).

"The smoke was at this time so dense that but little could be seen of the battle..." – General Gibbon describing the fight with Confederate artillery as Confederate infantry struck his division on Cemetery Ridge at dusk on July 2 (OR 417).

"Their color bearer fell, pierced by a dozen bullets" – Major Curtis, 7th Michigan, depicting the moment when Confederate attackers placed a flag atop abandoned Union guns as they got within 30 yards the Federal line on their way to storming the center of Cemetery Ridge on July 2 (OR 1: 447).

"Had it been successful, the result would have been terribly disastrous to our army and to the country" – General Slocum, XII Corps, regarding Longstreet's attack against the Union left (OR 1: 759).

"They advanced into the woods, where it was impossible to tell friend from foe, and before they scarcely knew it were in the midst of a brigade of the enemy" – Colonel Colgrove, Ruger's Brigade, reporting of Company F of the 2nd Massachusetts who served as skirmishers for the brigade upon its return to Culp's Hill on the night of July 2 (OR 1: 813).

"...we were very near a force of the enemy, as talking could be plainly heard..." – Colonel Morse, 2nd Massachusetts, describing his regiment's location at Spangler's Spring on the night of July 2 (OR 1: 817).

"The darkness was so great ... that we could not see the enemy, and we fired at the flashes of their guns. They were so close to us..." – Colonel Redington, 60th New York, referring to the late fighting on Culp's Hill (OR 1: 862).

July 3

"The next day, July 3, was the hottest of the battle, and this was the severest engagement of the war" – Colonel Rogers, 2nd Rhode Island (OR 1: 683).

"...no braver man ever took arms to vindicate his country's honor and uphold its glory, or was animated by purer and simpler patriotism" – Colonel Mausby, 1st Maryland Potomac, praising each of three officers lost from his regiment in the morning on Culp's Hill. He further wrote, "the gallantry of our lost brethren in arms, enlisted and commissioned, has embalmed their memories in the affections of their surviving comrades, while the sufferings of the wounded elicit their profoundest sympathies" (OR 1: 806-807).

"The enemy [were] charging heavily ... and yelling in their peculiar style" – General Geary, Culp's Hill, July 3 (OR 1: 828).

"Large numbers of them crawled under our breastworks and begged to be taken as prisoners" – General Geary describing the Confederates on Culp's Hill as Union forces finally overwhelmed them after seven and a half hours of morning fighting. When a Confederate officer raised a white flag in surrender, the assistant adjutant-general of that division, Major Leigh, "rode forward to order it down," only to fall, "pierced by a dozen balls" (OR 1: 830).

"The First Maryland Battalion (Confederate States) left most of their dead in line with our own. It cannot be denied that they behaved courageously" – General Kane, Kane's Brigade, regarding the last Confederate charge on Culp's Hill (OR 1: 847).

"About 1 o'clock ... the enemy opened upon our front with the heaviest artillery fire I have ever known" – General Hancock, II Corps, Cemetery Ridge, July 3 (OR 1: 372).

"The heaps and mounds of dead and wounded enemies which were found ... well satisfy the ambition for bloody deeds of each man of every regiment engaged" – Colonel Mausby, 1st Maryland Potomac, after fighting ceased on Culp's Hill (OR 1: 806).

"... the enemy opened upon us with all his artillery the most fearful fire I have ever witnessed" – General Caldwell, Caldwell's Division, regarding the afternoon cannonade of July 3. He subsequently stated, "although this lasted an hour, but one of my men was killed and very few wounded" (OR 1: 380).

"There was no place of safety" – General Howard regarding the condition on Cemetery Hill during the cannonade in which "missiles of every description", and from all directions, were concentrated on this spot. "Shells burst in the air, in the ground to the right and left, killing horses, exploding caissons, overturning tombstones, and smashing fences" (OR 1: 706).

"The enemy ... opened with a severity which good military judges have pronounced to be the severest artillery fire of the war" – Captain Burke, 88th New York, describing the cannonade of July 3 (OR 1: 391).

"The spectacle was magnificent" – Major Ellis, 14th CT, describing Pickett's Charge as he witnessed the immense lines of Confederates march across the fields (1: 467).

"...our artillery, which up to this time, had remained almost silent, opened with terrible effect ... tearing great gaps in their ranks and strewing the field with dead and wounded. Notwithstanding the destructive fire under which they were placed, the enemy continued to advance with a degree of ardor, coolness, and bravery worthy of a better cause..." – Major Mulholland, 116th PA, observations of Pickett's Charge (OR 1: 392).

"In claiming for my brigade and a few other troops the turning point of the battle of July 3, I do not forget how liable inferior commanders are to regard only what takes place in their own front ... [however] ... The decision of the rebel commander was upon that point; the concentration of artillery fire was upon that point; the din of battle developed in a column of attack upon that point; and the victory was at that point" – Colonel Hall, Hall's Brigade, claiming the honor due his men who resisted Pickett's Charge at the Copse (OR 1: 441).

"Lieut. A. H. Cushing, Fourth U.S. Artillery, fell, mortally wounded, at the fence by the side of his guns ... [having] fought for an hour and a half after he had reported to me that he was wounded in both thighs," – General Webb, Webb's Brigade, praising Cushing's performance at the Angle (OR 1: 429).

"For an instant it seemed to hang in the balance ..." – Colonel Devereux, 19th Mass., describing the intensity of the hand-to-hand fighting at the Angle (OR 1: 444).

"All seemed lost,...but on reaching the crest...the tide turned" – Captain Hazard, Hazard's Artillery, describing Armistead's thrust at the Angle (OR 1: 480).

"The Sixty-ninth Pennsylvania Volunteers lost all of its field officers, but held its ground. ... I saw none retire from the fence" – General Webb praising the best regiment of his brigade in the action at the Angle (OR 1: 428).

"...the ordinary brave man sees nothing but a tumult and remembers after it is over nothing but a whirl of events which he is unable to separate" – Captain Abbott, 20th Massachusetts, describing the effect of battle while reflecting on the conduct of his men during Pickett's Charge (OR 1: 446).

"He... was instantly killed, with one of the enemy's captured flags in his hand" – Colonel Smyth, Smyth's Brigade, regarding Lieutenant William Smith of the 1st Delaware who died at the front of his regiment in the hand-to-hand combat of Pickett's Charge (1: 466).

"... it was for most of them their first battle" – General Stannard, Stannard's Brigade, on his Vermont regiments that fought at the front against Pickett's Charge (OR 1: 350).

"The men assisted in maneuvering the guns when so many of the horses were killed..." Colonel Smyth, Smyth's Brigade, regarding the support his 108th New Yorkers gave to Woodruff's Battery during Pickett's Charge (1: 465).

"...there remained but 3 out of 13 officers" – Captain Abbott, 20th Massachusetts, reporting the losses of his regiment from fighting at the Copse of Trees during Pickett's Charge (OR 1: 446).

"The enemy must be short of ammunition, as I was shot with a tenpenny nail" – General Hancock, II Corps, in the aftermath of Pickett's Charge (OR 1: 366).

"Two battle-flags of the enemy were taken by men of my regiment, but were torn from the lances by men of other regiments" – Colonel Heath, 19th Maine, regarding their fight against Pickett's Charge (OR 1: 422).

"...the decisive and final infantry charge of General Longstreet ... have rendered this day historical" – Colonel Dana, 143rd Pennsylvania, July 3 (OR 1: 336).

"... the ground was literally black with killed and wounded" – Major Dent, 1st Delaware (OR 1: 470).

"The men by this time had become very much exhausted from previous long marches, constant watchfulness, and having been destitute of food nearly two days" – Major Curtis, 7th Michigan, evening of July 3 (OR 1: 450).

"The history of this brigade's operations is written in blood," – General Hays, Hays' Division, lamenting the losses sustained by his Third Brigade at Gettysburg under Colonel George Willard, who was killed in battle. Hays continued to write shockingly in his report, "The loss of this brigade [alone] amounts to one-half the casualties in the [entire] division" (OR 1: 453).

"The dead of both sides lay in lines in every direction" – General Crawford, Crawford's Division, describing the scene in the Wheatfield after his men gained final possession of it in the evening of July 3 (OR 1: 655).

"Among the list [of many brave and gallant officers lost] will be found the name of Farnsworth; short but most glorious was his career – a general on June 29, on the 30th he baptized his star in blood, and on July 3, for the honor of his young brigade and the glory of his corps, he gave his life. At the head of his men, at the very muzzles of the enemy's guns, he fell, with many mortal wounds. We can say of him, in the language of another, 'Good soldier, faithful friend, great heart, hail and farewell' " (OR 1: 993).

"As the operations of the cavalry are mostly on the exterior of the army and out of view of the greater part of it, but an imperfect knowledge exists of the importance and arduousness of its service" – Captain Tidball, Tidball's Horse Artillery Brigade, on the disadvantage of cavalry units in receiving due recognition (OR 1: 1028).

"All prisoners agree in saying that it was by far the most desperate battle of the war" –Lieutenant Haskell, 125th New York (OR 1: 477).

POST-BATTLE AND REFLECTION

"... the enemy, defeated and disheartened, had fled away…" – Major Willis, 119th New York, July 4 (OR 1: 743).

To "do honor to our native State, the old Keystone[, the] men [had been] unusually anxious to meet the enemy, … inspired with a feeling of do or die in the attempt to annihilate the invaders of their homes" – Major Bodine, 26th PA (OR 1: 556).

"I may safely add that the Second Brigade was the first to enter the town of Gettysburg after the battle," – Colonel Harris, 75th Ohio, July 4 (OR 1: 716).

"On the 4th, we buried our dead and held short religious services ..." – Major Bradley, 64th New York (OR 1: 406).

"The skill and gallantry with which [our guns] were handled [throughout the battle] is amply attested by the dead of the enemy, slain by shell and canister, ... and the fierce fire under which [my men] did their work is proved by the heavy loss of horses ..." – General Tyler, Artillery Reserve (OR 1: 874).

"All [felt] they were fighting on the soil of their native State, and ... would either conquer or yield up their lives in her defense" – Colonel Craig, 105th PA (OR 1: 502).

"In justice to the surviving officers and men … who have on many hard-fought battlefields distinguished themselves for gallantry and undaunted courage, I cannot close this report without expressing my admiration for their soldierly conduct on this occasion.

At the same time I may be permitted to express my deep and heartfelt sympathy for those who now mourn the loss of husbands, fathers, brothers, and friends, who have sacrificed their lives on the altar of their country in upholding its honor and integrity" (OR 1: 544-545).

"This charge ... was the most gallant ever made" – General Kilpatrick in his cavalry division report describing Major Weber's 6th Michigan cavalry charge against entrenched Confederates near Falling Waters, Maryland, on July 14 (OR 1: 990).

"The battle of Gettysburg is the decisive battle of this war," to the editor of the *New York Herald* from Historicus in March of 1864 (OR 1: 128).

"...the newspapers ... bearing upon the battle of Gettysburg ... [are] calculated to convey a wrong impression to your mind..." – General Howard to President Abraham Lincoln on July 18. Howard praised Meade's performance to Lincoln "because of the censure and of the misrepresentations which have grown out of the escape of Lee's army" (OR 1: 700).

"General Meade, justly the conqueror and hero of Gettysburg..." (1:221).

"I regret the loss of the many gallant patriots ... but I rejoice it was in the battle of Gettysburg and in defense of human freedom and republican institutions" – Colonel McFarland, 151st Pennsylvania (OR 1: 328-329).

Confederate Army of Northern Virginia

July 1

"The whereabouts of our army was still a mystery ..." – General J.E.B. Stuart, Cavalry Division, Dillsburg, PA, July 1 (OR 2: 697).

"...[Lee] did not want a general engagement brought on till the rest of the army came up" – General Ewell, II Corps, regarding orders received from Lee on July 1. But according to Ewell, "by the time this message reached me, General A. P. Hill had already been warmly engaged with a large body of the enemy" at Gettysburg (OR 2: 444).

"... 500 of my men were left lying dead and wounded on a line as straight as a dress parade..." – General Iverson describing the slaughter of his brigade on Oak Ridge where Union troops behind a stone wall had risen up and suprised his Confederates with devastating fire. The killing was so quick and powerful that those in his front battle line who escaped death fell down and raised white hankerchiefs in surrender (OR 2: 579).

"...the enemy's loss was five times as great as ours" – Captain Hillyer, 9th Georgia, indicating the magnitude of Confederate victory on the first day (OR 2: 401).

"...the remnants of what had been a fine Yankee flag were lying in different places" – Captain Hopkins, 45th North Carolina, describing what his troops found of the 16th Maine's flag after that regiment had torn it up to avoid the capture of their colors in the frantic Union retreat from Oak Ridge (OR 2: 575).

"A very large number of prisoners were captured in the town ... their number being so great as really to embarrass us" – General Jubal Early, Early's Division (OR 2: 469).

"The want of cavalry had been and was again seriously felt" – General Hill, III Corps, referring to J.E.B. Stuart's absence on the first day. Hill claimed that without Stuart's cavalry, he had been unable to ascertain the strength of Union forces at Gettysburg on June 30, which compelled him to send in Heth's men on July 1, and he again fretted over the absence of reconnaissance that he so badly wanted as his Corps cautiously pushed and followed retreating Union forces through the town of Gettysburg, not knowing what Federal reinforcements might lay in wake (OR 2: 607).

"...we captured more by far than the number of men in the command" – Colonel Grimes, 4th North Carolina, who claimed his regiment was "the first to enter the town of Gettysburg" in pursuit of retreating Union forces (OR 2: 590).

"The men being so much fatigued by the forced march ... the pursuit was discontinued" – Major Lambeth, 14th NC, whose men marched 14 miles to reach Gettysburg, and went immediately into battle, capturing "an immense number" of Union soldiers and driving more through town until exhaustion overcame them (OR 2: 590).

"Gettysburg was now completely in our possession" – Colonel Perrin, Perrin's Brigade, evening of July 1 (OR 2: 662).

July 2

"...we were ordered forward, and advanced ...[over] the worst cliffs of rocks there could have been traveled over" – Colonel Sheffield, 48th Alabama, on attacking Devil's Den (OR 2: 395).

"... the strongest natural position I ever saw" – Captain Hillyer, 9th GAa, referring to Little Round Top upon seeing it after his men helped take Houck's Ridge (OR 2: 399).

"...a mountain held by the enemy in heavy force with artillery ... was the key to the enemy's left" – General Robertson regarding Little Round Top which his brigade assaulted on July 2 (OR 2: 404).

"...a terrific fire of artillery was concentrated against the hill [Houck's Ridge] occupied by this regiment, and many were killed and wounded, some losing their heads, and others so horribly mutilated and mangled that their identity could scarcely be established..." – Colonel Work, 1st Texas, evening of July 2 (OR 2: 409).

"The colors were then taken by Sergt. Evans, of Company F, who planted them defiantly in the face of the foe ..." – Major Rogers, 5th Texas, describing the successive loss of color bearers during the assaults against Little Round Top (OR 2: 414).

"Having exhausted their original ... ammunition, the men supplied themselves from the cartridge-boxes of their dead and disabled comrades and from the dead and wounded of the enemy, frequently going in front of the hill to secure a cartridge-box" – Colonel Work, 1st Texas, whose men daringly ran into the Valley of Death for ammunition, risking fire from Little Round Top, during the evening of July 2 (OR 2: 410).

"The sound of the stones dropping into place could be distinctly heard from our line during the whole night" – General Benning, on hearing the construction of stone walls and breastworks on Little Round Top after the fighting stopped on July 2 (OR 2: 416).

The "rout of the enemy was vigorously pressed to the very foot of the mountain, up the sides of which the enemy fled in the greatest confusion. The loss of the enemy was here very great, his dead lying upon the field by the hundred. Nothing but the exhausted condition of the men prevented them from carrying the heights [of Little Round Top]" – Major McDaniel, 11th Georgia, describing the scene in the Valley of Death (OR 2: 401-402).

"The fire from our lines and from the enemy became incessant, rendering it necessary for us sometimes to pause and allow the smoke to clear away, in order to enable the gunners to take aim" – Colonel Cabell referring to his artillery battalion dueling with Union batteries at the Peach Orchard (OR 2: 375).

"I lost ... one of my best gunners. He was killed while in the act of sighting his guns. He never spoke after receiving the shot, walked a few steps from his piece, and fell dead" – Captain Taylor, Taylor's Battery, referring to Corporal William Ray in the artillery assault on the Peach Orchard (OR 2: 432).

"He had both legs broken above the knees ... His only words were, 'You can do me no good; I am killed; follow your piece" – Captain Taylor referring to one of his gunners, Corporal Joseph Lantz, who was injured mortally while moving cannon across Emmitsburg Road to the Peach Orchard in the wake of Sickles' retreat (OR 2: 432).

"We were now complete masters of the field, having gained the key, as it were, of the enemy's whole line" – General Wright referring to the moment his brigade seized the center of Cemetery Ridge on the evening of July 2 (OR 2: 623).

"All was confusion and disorder" – Captain Buckner, 44th Virginia, describing the fighting in the woods on Culp's Hill as darkness made "it impossible to distinguish friend from foe" (OR 2: 538).

"All had been done that it was possible to do" – General Johnson referring to his division's attack on Culp's Hill on July 2 (OR 2: 505).

"Thus stood affairs at nightfall, the 2nd: On the left and in the center, nothing gained; on the right, batteries and lines well advanced, the enemy meanwhile strengthening himself in a position naturally formidable and everywhere difficult of approach..." – General Pendleton, Chief of Artillery, summing up the progress of the Confederate Army (OR 2: 351).

July 3

"... it was a useless sacrifice of life to keep them longer under so galling a fire" – General Walker explaining his withdrawal of the Stonewall brigade from Culp's Hill on the morning of July 3 (OR 2: 519).

"... they retired stubbornly from the field, manifesting a willingness to hurl themselves upon the foe again, if so ordered" – Colonel Funk, 5th Virginia, whose men found themselves under "a murderous and enfilading fire" in the morning fight on Culp's Hill, and had "to give way" (OR 2: 527).

"The horses had all been killed, and lay harnessed to the piece" – Major Eshleman describing an abandoned Union gun found on the field (OR 2: 434).

"So mighty an artillery contest has perhaps never been waged..." – General Pendleton describing the afternoon cannonade on July 3 (OR 2: 352).

"In no previous battle of the war had we so much artillery engaged..." – General Wilcox, Wilcox's Brigade, regarding the cannonade. He further observed that despite the awesome barrage of shot and shell, "I do not believe a single battery of the enemy had been disabled so as to stop its fire," after which Pickett's Division advanced to their destruction (OR 2: 619).

"The commanding general [Lee] ... ordered [an] attack ... to be made directly at the enemy's main position, Cemetery Hill" – General Longstreet, I Corps, in his report claiming Cemetery Hill was the objective of Pickett's Charge (OR 2: 359).

A battery on Little Round Top "enfiladed nearly our entire line with fearful effect, sometimes as many as 10 men being killed and wounded by the bursting of a single shell" – Major Peyton, Garnett's Brigade, describing the fire they endured while crossing the fields during Pickett's Charge (OR 2: 386).

"Not a man in the division ... could I see" – General Wilcox describing how severely the artillery fire and smoke obscured Pickett's Division marching in front of his brigade as they crossed the fields against the Union center (OR 2: 620).

"Our line, much shattered, still kept up the advance until within 20 paces of the wall, when, for a moment, it recoiled under the terrific fire, [and then Kemper, Armistead, and the remaining soldiers] rushed forward ... to plant the Southern Banner on the walls of the enemy. His strongest and last line was instantly gained; the Confederate battle-flag waved over his defenses, and the fighting over the wall became hand to hand" – Major Peyton depicting the assault at the Angle (OR 2: 386).

"The identity of every regiment being entirely lost, and every regimental commander killed or wounded ... and those who were not killed or wounded were captured" – Major Peyton describing the cost of Pickett's Charge (OR 2: 386-387).

"...the regiment halted and retreated, losing more men than a glorious victory would have cost..." – General Jones referring to the 7th Virginia cavalry of his brigade at Fairfield, July 3 (OR 2: 752).

"Lieutenant Duncan ... was conspicuous for his daring, having sabered five Yankees, running his saber entirely through one, and twisting him from his horse" – Major Flournoy, 6th Virginia Cavalry, on the battle at Fairfield on July 3 (OR 2: 756).

Post-battle and Reflection

Gettysburg is "the hardest fought battle of the war in which I have been engaged..." – General Robertson in closing of his official report (OR 2: 406).

"... we have no friends who will tell of our success ... because all but the Sixth Regiment failed... [and so] I write this now for fear I will not live to write at leisure hereafter" – Major Samuel Tate, 6th North Carolina, having described his regiment's assault on East Cemetery Hill of July 2nd in a letter to North Carolina Governor Zebulon Vance dated July 8 (OR 2: 486-487).

"... and there ended the Pennsylvania Campaign" – General Rodes on the Confederate Army's recrossing of the Potomac River into Virginia on July 14 (OR 2: 559).

8

The Organization of the Armies

"Mentioning the names of a few would be doing an injustice to the rest ..."

Every unit which fought in the battle deserves mention. The *Official Records* carefully printed the organization of the armies to show all participating units. This is a useful reference as demonstrated on the battlefield by numerous tablets and markers indicating every Corps, Division, Brigade, and Regiment that participated in the Gettysburg Campaign. But while the *Official Records* contain 356 Union officer reports and 145 Confederate officer reports, these are not enough for a record from every participating unit. This chapter clearly reveals which units had considerable report coverage, and which did not.

Some units failed to submit reports because of the loss of officers in battle. Readers need to be aware that this slants the perspective on the battle as reported in the *Official Records* — the memories and accounts in the reports are from officers who survived well and safe enough to write, not from the dead and severely wounded. Thus, units who bore the brunt of the severest fighting and whose officer ranks were decimated often contributed the fewest reports. A good example and consequence of this absence of reports concerns Pickett's Charge. The Confederate perspective of that charge is severely hindered by the fact that no reports are found in the *Official Records* from General Armistead's entire brigade who spearheaded the famous charge. Armistead's men were annihilated in the attack, and the only officer reports of their fighting are from other witnesses outside of their unit, mostly by those from the opposing army.

Another fascinating aspect of the *Official Records* is the use of nicknames. Every unit had a nickname, and some units were more often referred to in reports, press, and battle histories by their nickname rather than their official army unit designation. The "Iron Brigade" and the "Louisiana Tigers" are two good examples of unit nicknames mentioned in officer reports as well as in newspapers and battle histories over the years. Readers should be aware of the units most often associated with these and other common nicknames as they read the *Official Records*.

To aid readers best, this chapter contains the order of battle with two key additions:

(1) Every unit with a report(s) in the *Official Records* is denoted with the citation following the officer's name, i.e.; **(OR 1: 199)**.

(2) Unit nicknames are given in parentheses.

Finally, all officers are listed for every unit according to the order of their command in battle. Please note that (**) indicates an officer who took command of the unit after the battle.

A mark of (*) indicates the officer did not command the unit but served as an adjutant.

Army of the Potomac

Maj. Gen. George G. Meade, commanding. **(OR 1:61)**

Headquarters

Provost Marshal General: Brig. Gen. Marsena R. Patrick **(OR 1:224)**
  93rd New York, Col. John S. Crocker
  8th United States (eight cos.), Capt. Edwin W. H. Read
  2nd Pennsylvania Cavalry, Col. R. Butler Price
  6th Pennsylvania Cavalry, Cos. E and I, Capt. James Starr
  Regular cavalry (detachments from 1st, 2nd, 5th, and 6th Regiments).
Signal Corps: Capt. Lemuel B. Norton **(OR 1:199)**
Guards and Orderlies: Oneida (New York) Cavalry, Capt. Daniel P. Mann
Artillery: Brig. Gen. Henry J. Hunt **(OR 1:228)**
Engineers: Brig. Gen. Henry Benham **(OR 1:226)**
  15th New York (three cos.), Maj. Walter L. Cassin
  50th New York, Col. William H. Pettes
  United States Battalion, Capt. George H. Mendell

First Corps
Maj. Gen. Abner Doubleday **(OR 1:243)**
Maj. Gen. John Newton **(OR 1:260)**

HEADQUARTERS
  1st Maine Cavalry, Co. L, Capt. Constantine Taylor

FIRST DIVISION
  Brig. Gen. James S. Wadsworth **(OR 1:265)**
First Brigade (The " Iron Brigade")
Brig. Gen. Solomon Meredith, Col. William W. Robinson
  19th Indiana, Col. Samuel J. Williams
  24th Michigan, Col. Henry Morrow **(OR 1:267)**, Capt. Albert Edwards
  2d Wisconsin, Col. Lucius Fairchild, Maj. John Mansfield **(OR 1:273)**,
    Capt. George H. Otis
  6th Wisconsin, Lt. Col. Rufus R. Dawes **(OR 1:275)**
  7th Wisconsin, Col. Wm. Robinson **(OR 1:278)**, Maj. Mark Finnicum
Second Brigade
Brig. Gen. Lysander Cutler **(OR 1:281)**
  7th Indiana, Col. Ira G. Grover **(OR 1:284)**
  76th New York, Maj. Andrew J. Grover, Capt. John E. Cook **(OR 1:285)**
  84th New York (14th Militia), Col. Edward B. Fowler **(OR 1:286)**
  95th New York, Col. George H. Biddle, Maj. Edward Pye **(OR 1:287)**
  147th New York, Lt. Col. Francis C. Miller, Maj. George Harney
  56th Pennsylvania (nine cos.), Col. J. William Hofmann **(OR 1:288)**

SECOND DIVISION
  Brig. Gen. John C. Robinson **(OR 1:289)**
First Brigade
Brig. Gen. Gabriel R. Paul, Col. Samuel H. Leonard, Col. Adrian R. Root,
  Col. Richard Coulter, Col. Peter Lyle, Col. Richard Coulter **(OR 1:292)**

16th Maine, Col. Charles W. Tilden, Maj. Archibald D. Leavitt,
   * Lieut. Col. Augustus Farnham **(OR 1:295)**
13th Massachusetts, Col. Samuel Leonard, Lt. Col. Walter Batchelder **(OR 1:297)**
94th New York, Col. Adrian R. Root, Maj. Samuel A. Moffett **(OR 1:299)**
104th New York, Col. Gilbert G. Prey **(OR 1:300)**
107th Pennsylvania, Lt. Col. James MacThomson **(OR 1:304)**,
   Capt. Emanuel D. Roath **(OR 1:305)**

Second Brigade
Brig. Gen. Henry Baxter **(OR 1:307)**
   12th Massachusetts, Col. James L. Bates, Lt. Col. David Allen, jr.
   83rd New York (9th Militia), Lieut. Col. Joseph A Moesch
   97th New York, Col. Charles Wheelock **(OR 1:309)**, Maj. Charles Northrup
   11th Pennsylvania, Col. Richard Coulter, Capt. Benjamin F. Haines,
      Capt. John B. Overmyer, ** Capt. Jacob J. Bierer **(OR 1:302)**
   88th Pennsylvania, Maj. Benezet F. Foust, Capt. Henry Whiteside,
      ** Capt. Edmund Y. Patterson **(OR 1:310)**
   90th Pennsylvania, Col. Peter Lyle, Maj. Alfred J. Sellers, Col. Peter Lyle

THIRD DIVISION
   Brig. Gen. Thomas A. Rowley **(OR 1:312)**, Maj. Gen. Abner Doubleday
First Brigade
Col. Chapman Biddle (OR 1:314), Brig. Gen. Thomas A. Rowley, Col. Chapman Biddle
   80th New York (20th Militia), Col. Theodore B. Gates **(OR 1:317)**
   121st Pennsylvania, Maj. Alexander Biddle **(OR 1:323)**,
      Col. Chapman Biddle, Maj. Alexander Biddle
   142nd Pennsylvania, Col. Robert P. Cummins, Lt. Col. A. McCalmont **(OR 1:325)**
   151st Pennsylvania, Lt. Col. George F. McFarland **(OR 1:326)**,
      Capt. Walter L. Owens, Col. Harrison Allen

Second Brigade
Col. Roy Stone **(OR 1:329)**, Col. Langhorne Wister **(OR 1:331)**,
   Col. Edmund L. Dana **(OR 1:334)**
   143rd Pennsylvania, Col. Edmund L. Dana, Lt. Col. John D. Musser **(OR 1:338)**
   149th Pennsylvania, Lt. Col. Walton Dwight **(OR 1:341)**,
      Capt. James Glenn, ** Capt. John Irvin **(OR 1:344)**
   150th Pennsylvania, Col. L. Wister, Lt. Col. H. Huidekoper **(OR 1:346)**
   Capt. Cornelius C. Widdis, ** Capt. George W. Jones **(OR 1:347)**

Third Brigade
Brig. Gen. George J. Stannard **(OR 1:348)**, Col. Francis V. Randall
   12th Vermont, Col. Asa P. Blunt
   13th Vermont, Col. Francis V. Randall **(OR 1:351)**,
      Maj. Joseph J. Boynton, Lieut. Col. William D. Munson
   14th Vermont, Col. William T. Nichols
   15th Vermont, Col. Redfield Proctor
   16th Vermont, Col. Wheelock G. Veazey **(OR 1:1041)**

Artillery Brigade
Col. Charles S. Wainwright **(OR 1:354)**
   Maine Light, 2nd Battery (B), Capt. James A. Hall **(OR 1:359)**
   Maine Light, 5th Battery (E), Capt. G. T. Stevens, Lt. E. Whittier **(OR 1:360)**
   1st New York Light, Battery L, Capt. G. Reynolds, Lt. G. Breck **(OR 1:362)**
   1st Pennsylvania Light, Battery B, Capt. James H. Cooper **(OR 1:364)**
   4th United States, Battery B, Lt. James Stewart

Second Corps
Maj. Gen. Winfield S. Hancock **(OR 1:366)**
Brig. Gen. John Gibbon

HEADQUARTERS
    6th New York Cavalry, Companies D and K, Capt. Riley Johnson

FIRST DIVISION
    Brig. Gen. John C. Caldwell **(OR 1:379)**

First Brigade
Col. Edward E. Cross, Col. H. Boyd McKeen **(OR 1:381)**
    5th New Hampshire, Lt. Col. C. Hapgood, **Maj. R. Cross **(OR 1:383)**
    61st New York, Lieut. Col. K. Oscar Broady **(OR 1:384)**
    81st Pennsylvania, Col. H. Boyd McKeen, Lt. Col. Amos Stroh **(OR 1:385)**
    148th Pennsylvania, Lt. Col. Robert McFarlane

Second Brigade (The "Irish Brigade")
Col. Patrick Kelly **(OR 1:386)**
    28th Massachusetts, Col. R. Byrnes **(OR 1:387)**
    63rd New York (two cos.), Lt. Col. R. Bentley, Capt. T. Touhy **(OR 1:387)**
    69th New York (two cos.), Capt. Richard Moroney, Lt. J. Smith **(OR 1:388)**
    88th New York (two cos.), Capt. Denis F. Burke **(OR 1:390)**
    116th Pennsylvania (four cos.), Maj. St. Clair A. Mulholland **(OR 1:391)**

Third Brigade
Brig. Gen. Samuel K. Zook, Lieut. Col. John Fraser **(OR 1:393)**
    52nd New York, Lt. Col. C. G. Freudenberg, Capt. Wm. Scherrer **(OR 1:395)**
    57th New York, Lt. Col. Alford B. Chapman **(OR 1:396)**
    66th New York, Col. Orlando H. Morris, Lt. Col. John S. Hammell,
        Maj. Peter Nelson **(OR 1:397)**
    140th Pennsylvania, Col. Richard P. Roberts, Lt. Col. John Fraser

Fourth Brigade
Col. John R. Brooke **(OR 1:399)**
    27th Connecticut (two cos.), Lt. Col. Henry Merwin, Maj. James Coburn
    2nd Delaware, Col. William Baily **(OR 1:402)**, Capt. Charles Christman
    64th New York, Col. Daniel Bingham, Maj. Leman Bradley **(OR 1:405)**
    53rd Pennsylvania, Lt. Col. Richards McMichael **(OR 1:409)**
    145th Pennsylvania (seven cos.), Col. Hiram L. Brown,
        Capt. John W. Reynolds **(OR 1:413)**, Capt. Moses W. Oliver **(OR 1:415)**

SECOND DIVISION
    Brig. Gen. John Gibbon **(OR 1:416)**, Brig. Gen. William Harrow **(OR 1:419)**

First Brigade
Brig. Gen. William Harrow, Col. Francis E. Heath
    19th Maine, Col. Francis Heath **(OR 1:422)**, Lt. Col. Henry Cunningham
    15th Massachusetts, Col. George Ward, Lt. Col. George Joslin **(OR 1:423)**
    1st Minnesota, Col. William Colvill, Jr., Capt. Nathan S. Messick
        Capt. Henry C. Coates **(OR 1:424)**
    82nd New York, Lt. Col. James Huston, Capt. John Darrow **(OR 1:426)**

Second Brigade (The "Philadelphia Brigade")
Brig. Gen. Alexander S. Webb **(OR 1:427)**
    69th Pennsylvania, Col. Dennis O'Kane, Capt. William Davis **(OR 1:430)**
    71st Pennsylvania, Col. Richard Penn Smith **(OR 1:432)**
    72nd Pennsylvania, Col. De Witt Baxter, Lt. Col. Theo. Hesser **(OR 1:433)**
    106th Pennsylvania, Lt. Col. William L. Curry **(OR 1:433)**

Third Brigade
Col. Norman J. Hall **(OR 1:435)**
    19th Massachusetts, Col. Arthur F. Devereux **(OR 1:442)**
    20th Massachusetts, Col. Paul J. Revere, Lt. Col. George N. Macy,
        Capt. Henry L. Abbott **(OR 1:445)**
    7th Michigan, Lt. Col. Amos E. Steele, Jr., Maj. Sylvanus W. Curtis **(OR 1:447)**
    42nd New York, Col. James E. Mallon **(OR 1:451)**
    59th New York (four cos.), Lt. Col. Max A. Thoman,
        Capt. William McFadden **(OR 1:452)**
Unattached
    Mass. Sharpshooters, 1st Co., Capt. William Plumer, Lt. Emerson L. Bicknell

THIRD DIVISION
    Brig. Gen. Alexander Hays **(OR 1:453)**
First Brigade
Col. Samuel S. Carroll **(OR 1:456)**
    14th Indiana, Col. John Coons **(OR 1:458)**, *Capt. Nathan Willard **(OR 1:459)**
    4th Ohio, Lt. Col. Leonard W. Carpenter **(OR 1:460)**
    8th Ohio, Lt. Col. Franklin Sawyer **(OR 1:461)**
    7th West Virginia, Lt. Col. Jonathan H. Lockwood **(OR 1:463)**
Second Brigade
Col. Thomas A. Smyth **(OR 1:464)**, Lt. Col. Francis E. Pierce
    14th Connecticut, Maj. Theodore G. Ellis **(OR 1:466)**
    1st Delaware, Lt. Col. Edward P. Harris, Capt. Thomas B. Hizar,
        Lt. William Smith, Lt. John T. Dent **(OR 1:468)**
    12th New Jersey, Maj. John T. Hill **(OR 1:470)**
    10th New York (battalion), Maj. George F. Hopper **(OR 1:471)**
    108th New York, Lt. Col. Francis E. Pierce
Third Brigade
Col. George L. Willard, Col. Eliakim Sherrill, Lt. Col. James M. Bull **(OR 1:472)**
    39th New York (four companies), Maj. Hugo Hildebrandt
    111th New York, Col. Clinton D. MacDougall **(OR 1:474)**,
        Lt. Col. Isaac M. Lusk, Capt. Aaron P. Seeley **(OR 1:475)**
    125th New York, Lt. Col. Levin Crandell, *Lt. Harry L. Haskell **(OR 1:477)**
    126th New York, Col. Eliakim Sherill, Lt. Col. James M. Bull
Artillery Brigade
Capt. John G. Hazard **(OR 1:477)**
    1st New York Light, Battery B, Lt. Albert S. Sheldon, Capt. James M. Rorty,
        Lt. Roberts E. Rogers
    1st Rhode Island Light, Battery A, Capt. William A. Arnold
    1st Rhode Island Light, Battery B, Lt. T. Fred Brown, Lt. Walter S. Perrin
    1st United States, Battery I, Lt. George A. Woodruff, Lt. Tully McCrea
    4th United States, Battery A, Lt. Alonzo H. Cushing, Sgt. Frederick Ruger

Third Corps
Maj. Gen. Daniel Sickles, Maj. Gen. David Birney,
*Maj. Gen. William French **(OR 1:488)**

FIRST DIVISION
    Maj. Gen. David B. Birney **(OR 1:482)**, Brig. Gen. J. H. Hobart Ward
First Brigade
Brig. Gen. Charles K. Graham, Col. Andrew H. Tippin

57th Pennsylvania (eight cos.), Col. Peter Sides, Capt. Alanson Nelson **(OR 1:497)**
63rd Pennsylvania, Maj. John A. Danks **(OR 1:498)**
68th Pennsylvania, Col. Andrew H. Tippin **(OR 1:498)**, Capt. Milton S. Davis
105th Pennsylvania, Col. Calvin A. Craig **(OR 1:500)**
114th Pennsylvania, Lt. Col. Frederick Cavada, Capt. Edward Bowen **(OR 1:502)**
141st Pennsylvania, Col. Henry J. Madill **(OR 1:504)**
Second Brigade
Brig. Gen. J. H. Hobart Ward **(OR 1:493)**, Col. Hiram Berdan
    20th Indiana, Col. John Wheeler, Lt. Col. William Taylor **(OR 1:506)**
    3rd Maine, Col. Moses B. Lakeman **(OR 1:507)**
    4th Maine, Col. Elijah Walker, Capt. Edwin Libby **(OR 1:510)**,
        *Lieut. Charles F. Sawyer **(OR 1:509)**
    86th New York, Lieut. Col. Benjamin L. Higgins **(OR 1:511)**
    124th New York, Col. A. Van Horne Ellis, Lt. Col. Francis Cummins **(OR 1:512)**
    99th Pennsylvania, Maj. John W. Moore **(OR 1:513)**
    1st United States Sharpshooters, Col. Hiram Berdan **(OR 1:514)**,
        Lt. Col. Casper Trepp **(OR 1:516)**
    2nd U.S. Sharpshooters (eight cos.), Maj. Homer Stoughton **(OR 1:518)**
Third Brigade
Col. P. Regis De Trobriand **(OR 1:519)**
    17th Maine, Lt. Col. Charles B. Merrill **(OR 1:522)**
    3rd Michigan, Col. Byron R. Pierce, Lt. Col. Edwin S. Pierce **(OR 1:523)**
    5th Michigan, Lieut. Col. John Pulford **(OR 1:525)**
    40th New York, Col. Thomas W. Egan **(OR 1:526)**
    110th Pennsylvania (six cos.), Lt. Col. David M. Jones,
        Maj. Isaac Rogers **(OR 1:528)**

SECOND DIVISION
    Brig. Gen. A. A. Humphreys **(OR 1:529)**, **Brig. Gen. H. Prince **(OR 1:537)**
First Brigade
Brig. Gen. Joseph B. Carr **(OR 1:541)**
    1st Massachusetts, Lt. Col. Clark B. Baldwin **(OR 1:547)**
    11th Massachusetts, Lt. Col. Porter D. Tripp **(OR 1:548)**
    16th Massachusetts, Lt. Col. W. Merriam, Capt. M. Donovan **(OR 1:550)**
    12th New Hampshire, Capt. John F. Langley
    11th New Jersey, Col. Robert McAllister **(OR 1:551)**, Capt. Luther Martin,
        Lt. John Schoonover **(OR 1:553)**, Capt. William H. Lloyd,
        Capt. Samuel Sleeper, Lt. John Schoonover, *Capt. Wm. Dunning **(OR 1:555)**
    26th Pennsylvania, Maj. Robert L. Bodine **(OR 1:555)**
    84th Pennsylvania, Lt. Col. Milton Opp **(OR 1:557)**
Second Brigade (The "Excelsior Brigade")
Col. William R. Brewster **(OR 1:558)**
    70th New York, Col. J. Egbert Farnum, *Maj. William H. Hugo **(OR 1:562)**
    71st New York, Col. Henry L. Potter **(OR 1:564)**
    72nd New York, Col. John S. Austin **(OR 1:565)**, Lt. Col. John Leonard
    73rd New York, Maj. Michael W. Burns
    74th New York, Lt. Col. Thomas Holt
    120th New York, Lt. Col. Cornelius D. Westbrook, Maj. John R. Tappen,
        *Capt. Abram L. Lockwood **(OR 1:568)**
Third Brigade
Col. George C. Burling **(OR 1:569)**
    2nd New Hampshire, Col. Edward L. Bailey **(OR 1:573)**

5th New Jersey, Col. William J. Sewell **(OR 1:576)**,
    Capt. Thomas C. Godfrey, Capt. Henry H. Woolsey **(OR 1:575)**
6th New Jersey, Lt. Col. Stephen R. Gilkyson **(OR 1:577)**
7th New Jersey, Col. Louis R. Francine, Maj. Frederick Cooper **(OR 1:578)**
8th New Jersey, Col. John Ramsey, Capt. John G. Langston
115th Pennsylvania, Maj. John P. Dunne
Artillery Brigade
Capt. George E. Randolph **(OR 1:581)**, Capt. A. Judson Clark
    New Jersey Light, 2nd Battery, Capt. A. Judson Clark **(OR 1:585)**, Lt. Robert Sims
    1st New York Light, Battery D, Capt. George B. Winslow **(OR 1:586)**
    New York Light, 4th Battery, Capt. James E. Smith **(OR 1:588)**
    1st Rhode Island, Battery E, Lt. John Bucklyn, Lt. Benj. Freeborn **(OR 1:589)**
    4th U.S., Battery K, Lt. Francis W. Seeley, Lt. Robert James **(OR 1:590)**

Fifth Corps
Maj. Gen. George Sykes **(OR 1:592)**

HEADQUARTERS
    12th New York Infantry, (two cos.), Capt. Henry W. Rider
    17th Pennsylvania Cavalry, (two cos.), Capt. William Thompson
FIRST DIVISION
    Brig. Gen. James Barnes **(OR 1:598)**, **Brig. Gen. Charles Griffin **(OR 1:605)**
First Brigade
Col. William Tilton **(OR 1:607)**
    18th Massachusetts, Col. Joseph Hayes
    22nd Massachusetts, Lt. Col. Thomas Sherwin, Jr.
    1st Michigan, Col. Ira C. Abbott, Lt. Col. William A. Throop
    118th Pennsylvania, Lieut. Col. James Gwyn
Second Brigade
Col. Jacob B. Sweitzer **(R 1:608)**
    9th Massachusetts, Col. Patrick R. Guiney
    32nd Massachusetts, Col. G. L. Prescott
    4th Michigan, Col. Harrison H. Jeffords, Lt. Col. George W. Lumbard
    62nd Pennsylvania, Lt. Col. James C. Hull
Third Brigade
Col. Strong Vincent **(OR 1:613)**, Col. James C. Rice **(OR 1:615)**
    20th Maine, Col. Joshua L. Chamberlain **(OR 1:622)**,
        Capt. Atherton W. Clark **(OR 1:626)
    16th Michigan, Lt. Col. Norval E. Welch **(OR 1:627)**,
        Maj. Robert T. Elliott **(OR 1:628)
    44th New York, Col. James C. Rice, Lt. Col. Freeman Connor **(OR 1:630)**
    83rd Pennsylvania, Capt. Orpheus S. Woodward **(OR 1:632)**,
        Maj. William H. Lamont **(OR 1:632)
SECOND DIVISION
    Brig. Gen. Romeyn B. Ayres **(OR 1:634)**
First Brigade
Col. Hannibal Day **(OR 1:636)**
    3rd U.S. (six cos.), Capt. Henry W. Freedley, Capt. Richard G. Lay,
        Capt. Andrew Sheridan **(OR 1:637)
    4th U.S. (four cos.), Capt. Julius W. Adams, Jr. **(OR 1:638)**
    6th U.S. (five cos.), Capt. Levi C. Bootes **(OR 1:639)**

12th U.S. (eight cos.), Capt. Thomas S. Dunn **(OR 1:640)**
14th U.S. (eight cos.), Maj. Grotius R. Giddings **(OR 1:643)**
Second Brigade
Col. Sidney Burbank (OR 1:644)
    2nd U.S. (six cos.), Maj. Arthur T. Lee **(OR 1:646)**, Capt. Samuel A. McKee
    7th U.S. (four cos.), Capt. David P. Hancock **(OR 1:647)**
    10th U.S. (three cos.), Capt. William Clinton **(OR 1:648)**
    11th U.S. (six cos.), Maj. De Lancey Floyd-Jones **(OR 1:649)**
    17th U.S. (seven cos.), Lt. Col. J. Durell Greene **(OR 1:650)**
Third Brigade
Brig. Gen. Stephen H. Weed, Col. Kenner Garrard **(OR 1:651)**
    140th New York, Col. Patrick H. O'Rorke, Lt. Col. Louis Ernst
    146th New York, Col. Kenner Garrard, Lt. Col. David T. Jenkins
    91st Pennsylvania, Lt. Col. Joseph H. Sinex
    155th Pennsylvania, Lt. Col. John H. Cain

THIRD DIVISION (THE "PENNSYLVANIA RESERVES")
    Brig. Gen. Samuel W. Crawford **(OR 1:652)**
First Brigade
Col. William McCandless **(OR 1:657)**
    1st Pennslvania Reserves (nine cos.), Col. William C. Talley
    2nd Pennsylvania Reserves, Lt. Col. George A. Woodward
    6th Pennsylvania Reserves, Lt. Col. Wellington H. Ent
    13th Pennsylvania Reserves, Col. Charles Taylor, Maj. William Hartshorne
Third Brigade
Col. Joseph W. Fisher **(OR 1:658)**
    5th Pennsylvania Reserves, Lt. Col. George Dare
    9th Pennsylvania Reserves, Lt. Col. James McK. Snodgrass
    10th Pennsylvania Reserves, Col. Adoniram J. Warner
    11th Pennsylvania Reserves, Col. Samuel M. Jackson
    12th Pennsylvania Reserves (nine cos.), Col. Martin D. Hardin
Artillery Brigade
Capt. Augustus P. Martin **(OR 1:659)**
    Massachusetts Light, 3d Battery (C), Lt. Aaron F. Walcott
    1st New York Light, Battery C, Capt. Almont Barnes
    1st Ohio Light, Battery L, Capt. Frank C. Gibbs **(OR 1:662)**
    5th U.S., Battery D, Lt. Charles E. Hazlett, Lt. Benjamin F. Rittenhouse
    5th U.S., Battery I, Lt. Malbone F. Watson, Lt. Charles C. MacConnell

Sixth Corps
Maj. Gen. John Sedgwick **(OR 1:663)**

HEADQUARTERS
    1st New Jersey Cavalry, Company L,
    1st Pennsylvania Cavalry, Company H, Capt. William S. Craft
PROVOST GUARD
    4th New Jersey (three cos.), Capt. William R. Maxwell
FIRST DIVISION
    Brig. Gen. Horatio G. Wright **(OR 1:665)**
First Brigade (The "New Jersey Brigade")
Brig. Gen. A. T. A. Torbert **(OR 1:668)**
    1st New Jersey, Lt. Col. William Henry, Jr.

2nd New Jersey, Lt. Col. Charles Wiebecke
3rd New Jersey, Lt. Col. Edward L. Campbell
15th New Jersey, Col. William H. Penrose
Second Brigade
Brig. Gen. Joseph J. Bartlett **(OR 1:671)**
    5th Maine, Col. Clark S. Edwards
    121st New York, Col. Emory Upton **(OR 1:673)**
    95th Pennsylvania, Lt. Col. Edward Carroll
    96th Pennsylvania, Maj. William H. Lessig
Third Brigade
Brig. Gen. David A. Russell **(OR 1:673)**
    6th Maine, Col. Hiram Burnham
    49th Pennsylvania (four cos.), Lt. Col. Thomas M. Hulings
    119th Pennsylvania, Col. Peter C. Ellmaker
    5th Wisconsin, Col. Thomas S. Allen

SECOND DIVISION
    Brig. Gen. Albion P. Howe **(OR 1:675)**
Second Brigade (The "Vermont Brigade")
Col. Lewis A. Grant **(OR 1:676)**
    2nd Vermont, Col. James H. Walbridge
    3rd Vermont, Col. Thomas O. Seaver
    4th Vermont, Col. Charles B. Stoughton
    5th Vermont, Lt. Col. John R. Lewis
    6th Vermont, Col. Elisha L. Barney
Third Brigade
Brig. Gen. Thomas H. Neill **(OR 1:678)**
    7th Maine (six cos.), Lt. Col. Selden Connor
    33rd New York (detachment), Capt. Henry J. Gifford
    43rd New York, Lt. Col. John Wilson
    49th New York, Col. Daniel D. Bidwell
    77th New York, Lt. Col. Winsor B. French
    61st Pennsylvania, Lt. Col. George F. Smith

THIRD DIVISION
    Maj. Gen. John Newton, Brig. Gen. Frank Wheaton
First Brigade
Brig. Gen. Alexander Shaler **(OR 1:680)**
    65th New York, Col. Joseph E. Hamblin
    67th New York, Col. Nelson Cross
    122nd New York, Col. Silas Titus
    23rd Pennsylvania, Lt. Col. John F. Glenn
    82nd Pennsylvania, Col. Isaac C. Bassett
Second Brigade
Col. Henry L. Eustis
    7th Massachusetts, Lt. Col. Franklin P. Harlow
    10th Massachusetts, Lt. Col. Joseph B. Parsons
    37th Massachusetts, Col. Oliver Edwards
    2nd Rhode Island, Col. Horatio Rogers, Jr. **(OR 1:683)**
Third Brigade
Brig. Gen. Frank Wheaton, Col. David J. Nevin **(OR 1:684)**
    62nd New York, Col. David J. Nevin, Lt. Col. Theodore B. Hamilton
    93rd Pennsylvania, Maj. John I. Nevin

98th Pennsylvania, Maj. John B. Kohler **(OR 1:686)**
102nd Pennsylvania, Col. John W. Patterson **(OR 1:687)**
139th Pennsylvania, Col. Frederick Collier, Lt. Col. William Moody **(OR 1:687)**
Artillery Brigade
Col. Charles H. Tompkins
    Massachusetts Light, 1st Battery (A), Capt. William McCartney **(OR 1:688)**
    New York Light, 1st Battery, Capt. Andrew Cowan **(OR 1:689)**
    New York Light, 3d Battery, Capt. William A. Harn **(OR 1:691)**
    1st Rhode Island Light, Battery C, Capt. Richard Waterman **(OR 1:693)**
    1st Rhode Island Light, Battery G, Capt. George W. Adams **(OR 1:694)**
    2nd U.S., Battery D, Lieut. Edward B. Williston
    2nd U.S., Battery G, Lieut. John H. Butler
    5th U.S., Battery F, Lieut. Leonard Martin

Eleventh Corps
Maj. Gen. Oliver O. Howard **(OR 1:696)**

HEADQUARTERS
    1st Indiana Cavalry, (two cos.), Capt. Abram Sharra
    8th New York Infantry (one co.), Lt. Hermann Foerster

FIRST DIVISION
    Brig. Gen. Francis C. Barlow, Brig. Gen. Adelbert Ames **(OR 1:712)**
First Brigade
Col. Leopold Von Gilsa
    41st New York (nine cos.), Lt. Col. Detleo von Einsiedel **(OR 1:713)**
    54th New York, Maj. Stephen Kovacs, Lt. Ernst Both
    68th New York, Col. Gotthilf Bourry
    153rd Pennsylvania, Maj. John F. Frueauff
Second Brigade
Brig. Gen. Adelbert Ames, Col. Andrew L. Harris **(OR 1:715)**
    17th Connecticut, Lt. Col. Douglas Fowler, Maj. Allen G. Brady **(OR 1:716)**
    25th Ohio, Lt. Col. Jeremiah Williams, Capt. Nathaniel J. Manning,
        Lt. William Maloney, Lt. Israel White **(OR 1:719)**
    75th Ohio, Col. Andrew L. Harris, Capt. George B. Fox
    107th Ohio, Col. Seraphim Meyer, Capt. John M. Lutz **(OR 1:720)**

SECOND DIVISION
    Brig. Gen. Adolph Von Steinwehr **(OR 1:720)**
First Brigade
Col. Charles R. Coster
    134th New York, Lt. Col. Allan H. Jackson
    154th New York, Lt. Col. D. B. Allen
    27th Pennsylvania, Lt. Col. Lorenz Cantador
    73rd Pennsylvania, Capt. D. F. Kelley.
Second Brigade
Col. Orland Smith **(OR 1:723)**
    33rd Massachusetts, Col. Adin B. Underwood
    136th New York, Col. James Wood, jr. **(OR 1:725)**
    55th Ohio, Col. Charles B. Gambee
    73rd Ohio, Lt. Col. Richard Long

THIRD DIVISION
    Maj. Gen. Carl Schurz **(OR 1:727)**

First Brigade
Brig. Gen. Alexander Schimmelfennig, Col. George von Amsberg,
 **Brig. Gen. Hector Tyndale (OR 1:732)
  82nd Illinois, Lt. Col. Edward S. Salomon, **Col. Frederick Hecker (OR 1:734)
  45th New York, Col. George von Amsberg, Lt. Col. Adolphus Dobke (OR 1:735)
  157th New York, Col. Philip P. Brown, Jr. (OR 1:738)
  61st Ohio, Col. Stephen J. McGroarty
  74th Pennsylvania, Col. Adolph von Hartung, Lt. Col. Alexander von Mitzel,
   Capt. Gustav Schleiter, Capt. Henry Krauseneck

Second Brigade
Col. W. Krzyzanowski
  58th New York, Lt. Col. August Otto, Capt. Emil Koenig (OR 1:739)
  119th New York, Col. John T. Lockman, Lt. Col. Edward F. Lloyd,
   **Maj. Benjamin A. Willis (OR 1:742)
  82nd Ohio, Col. James S. Robinson, Lt. Col. David Thomson (OR 1:744)
  75th Pennsylvania, Col. Francis Mahler, Maj. August Ledig (OR 1:745)
  26th Wisconsin, Lt. Col. Hans Boebel, Capt. John W. Fuchs,
   **Col. William H. Jacobs (OR 1:746)

Artillery Brigade
Maj. Thomas W. Osborn (OR 1:747)
  1st New York Light, Battery I, Capt. Michael Wiedrich (OR 1:751)
  New York Light, 13th Battery, Lieut. William Wheeler (OR 1:752)
  1st Ohio Light, Battery I, Capt. Hubert Dilger (OR 1:754)
  1st Ohio Light, Battery K, Capt. Lewis Heckman (OR 1:755)
  4th U.S., Battery G, Lt. Bayard Wilkeson, Lt. Eugene A. Bancroft (OR 1:756),
   **Lt. Christopher F. Merkle (OR 1:757)

Twelfth Corps
Maj. Gen. Henry W. Slocum (OR 1:758)
Brig. Gen. Alpheus S. Williams (OR 1:770)

PROVOST GUARD
  10th Maine (four cos.), Capt. John D. Beardsley

FIRST DIVISION
  Brig. Gen. Alpheus S. Williams, Brig. Gen. Thomas H. Ruger (OR 1:777)
First Brigade
Col. Archibald L. McDougall (OR 1:782)
  5th Connecticut, Col. W. W. Packer (OR 1:788)
  20th Connecticut, Lieut. Col. William B. Wooster (OR 1:793)
  3rd Maryland, Col. J. Sudsburg (OR 1:795), **Lt. Col. G. Robinson (OR 1:796)
  123rd New York, Lt. Col. James Rogers (OR 1:797), Capt. Adolphus Tanner
  145th New York, Col. E. Livingston Price (OR 1:799)
  46th Pennsylvania, Col. James L. Selfridge (OR 1:802)

Second Brigade
Brig. Gen. Henry H. Lockwood (OR 1:804)
  1st Maryland, Potomac Home Brigade, Col. William P. Maulsby (OR 1:805)
  1st Maryland, Eastern Shore, Col. James Wallace (OR 1:808)
  150th New York, Col. John H. Ketcham (OR 1:809)

Third Brigade
Brig. Gen. Thomas H. Ruger, Col. Silas Colgrove (OR 1:810)
  27th Indiana, Col. Silas Colgrove, Lt. Col. John R. Fesler (OR 1:815)
  2nd Massachusetts, Lt. Col. Charles Mudge, Maj. Charles Morse (OR 1:816)

13th New Jersey, Col. Ezra A. Carman, **Lt. Col. John Grimes **(OR 1:818)**
107th New York, Col. Nirom M. Crane **(OR 1:819)**
3rd Wisconsin, Col. William Hawley **(OR 1:823)**

SECOND DIVISION
   Brig. Gen. John W. Geary **(OR 1:824)**
First Brigade
Col. Charles Candy **(OR 1:835)**
   5th Ohio, Col. John H. Patrick **(OR 1:839)**
   7th Ohio, Col. William R. Creighton **(OR 1:840)**
   29th Ohio, Capt. Wilbur Stevens **(OR 1:841)**, Capt. Edward Hayes **(OR 1:843)**
   66th Ohio, Lieut. Col. Eugene Powell **(OR 1:844)**
   28th Pennsylvania, Capt. John Flynn **(OR 1:845)**
   147th Pennsylvania (eight cos.), Lieut. Col. Ario Pardee, Jr. **(OR 1:845)**
Second Brigade
Col. George A. Cobham, Jr. **(OR 1:848)**, Brig. Gen. Thomas L. Kane **(OR 1:846)**,
   Col. George A. Cobham, Jr.
   29th Pennsylvania, Col. William Rickards, Jr. **(OR 1:851)**
   109th Pennsylvania, Capt. F. L. Gimber **(OR 1:853)**
   111th Pennsylvania, Lt. Col. Thomas M. Walker **(OR 1:854)**,
      Col. George A. Cobham, Jr., Lt. Col. Thomas M. Walker
Third Brigade
Brig. Gen. George S. Greene **(OR 1:855)**
   60th New York, Col. Abel Godard **(OR 1:860)**,
      *Lt. Col. John Redington **(OR 1:862)**
   78th New York, Lt. Col. Herbert von Hammerstein **(OR 1:863)**
   102nd New York, Col. James C. Lane, Capt. Lewis R. Stegman **(OR 1:864)**
   137th New York, Col. David Ireland **(OR 1:866)**
   149th New York, Col. Henry Barnum **(OR 1:867)**, Lt. Col. Charles Randall
Artillery Brigade
Lt. Edward D. Muhlenberg **(OR 1:869)**
   1st New York Light, Battery M, Lt. Charles E. Winegar
   Pennsylvania Light, Battery E, Lt. Charles A. Atwell ("Knap's Battery")
   4th U.S., Battery F, Lieut. Sylvanus T. Rugg
   5th U.S., Battery K, Lieut. David H. Kinzie

Cavalry Corps
Maj. Gen. Alfred Pleasonton **(OR 1:902)**

FIRST DIVISION
   Brig. Gen. John Buford **(OR 1:920)**
First Brigade
Col. William Gamble **(OR 1:932)**
   8th Illinois, Maj. John L. Beveridge
   12th Illinois (four cos.), 3rd Indiana (six cos.), Col. George H. Chapman
   8th New York, Lt. Col. William L. Markell
Second Brigade
Col. Thomas C. Devin **(OR 1:938)**
   6th New York, Maj. William E. Beardsley
   9th New York, Col. William Sackett
   17th Pennsylvania, Col. J. H. Kellogg
   3rd West Virginia (two cos.), Capt. Seymour B. Conger

Reserve Brigade
Brig. Gen. Wesley Merritt **(OR 1:943)**
    6th Pennsylvania, Maj. James H. Haseltine
    1st U.S., Capt. Richard S. C. Lord.
    2nd U.S., Capt T. F. Rodenbough
    5th U.S., Capt. Julius W. Mason **(OR 1:946)**
    6th U.S., Maj. Samuel H. Starr, Lt. Louis H. Carpenter,
        Lt. Nicholas Nolan **(OR 1:948)**, Capt. Ira W. Claflin

SECOND DIVISION
    Brig. Gen. David McM. Gregg **(OR 1:949)**
Headquarters Guard
    1st Ohio, Company A, Capt. Noah Jones
First Brigade
Col. John B. McIntosh **(OR 1:967, 1050)**
    1st Maryland (eleven cos.), Lt. Col. James M. Deems
    Purnell (Maryland) Legion, Company A, Capt. Robert E. Duvall
    1st Massachusetts, Lt. Col. Greely S. Curtis
    1st New Jersey, Maj. M. H. Beaumont
    1st Pennsylvania, Col. John P. Taylor
    3rd Pennsylvania, Lt. Col. E. S. Jones
    3rd Pennsylvania Heavy Artillery, Battery H, Capt. W. D. Rank
Second Brigade
Col. Pennock Huey **(OR 1:970)**
    2nd New York, Lt. Col. Otto Harhaus
    4th New York, Lt. Col. Augustus Pruyn
    6th Ohio (ten cos.), Maj. William Stedman **(OR 1:972)**
    8th Pennsylvania, Capt. William A. Corrie **(OR 1:973)**
Third Brigade
Col. J. Irvin Gregg **(OR 1:974)**
    1st Maine, Lt. Col. Charles H. Smith **(OR 1:979, 1057)**
    10th New York, Maj. M. Henry Avery **(OR 1:981)**
    4th Pennsylvania, Lt. Col. William E. Doster **(OR 1:983, 1058)**
    16th Pennsylvania, Lt. Col. John K. Robison

THIRD DIVISION
    Brig. Gen. Judson Kilpatrick **(OR 1:985)**
Headquarters Guard
    1st Ohio, Company C, Capt. Samuel N. Stanford
First Brigade
Brig. Gen. Elon J. Farnsworth, Col. Nathaniel P. Richmond **(OR 1:1005)**
    5th New York, Maj. John Hammond **(OR 1:1008)**
    18th Pennsylvania, Lt. Col. Wm. Brinton, **Maj. Wm. Darlington **(OR 1:1011)**
    1st Vermont, Lt. Col. Addison W. Preston **(OR 1:1012)**,
        Col. Edward B. Sawyer **(OR 1:1016)
    1st West Virginia, Col. Nathaniel Richmond, Maj. Charles Capehart **(OR 1:1018)**
Second Brigade
Brig. Gen. George A. Custer **(OR 1:997)**
    1st Michigan, Col. Charles H. Town
    5th Michigan, Col. Russell A. Alger
    6th Michigan, Col. George Gray
    7th Michigan, Col. William D. Mann

HORSE ARTILLERY
First Brigade
Capt. James M. Robertson **(OR 1:1020)**
    9th Michigan Battery, Capt. Jabez J. Daniels **(OR 1:1022)**
    6th New York Battery, Capt. Joseph W. Martin **(OR 1:1023)**
    2nd United States, Batteries B and L, Lt. Edward Heaton
    2nd United States, Battery M, Lt. A. C. M. Pennington, jr.
    4th United States, Battery E, Lt. Samuel S. Elder
Second Brigade
Capt. John C. Tidball **(OR 1:1028)**
    1st United States, Batteries E and G, Capt. Alanson M. Randol
    1st United States, Battery K, Capt. William M. Graham **(OR 1:1029)**
    2nd United States, Battery A, Lt. John H. Calef **(OR 1:1029)**
    3rd United States, Battery C, Lt. William D. Fuller **(OR 1:1034)**

Artillery Reserve
Brig. Gen. Robert O. Tyler **(OR 1:871)**
Capt. James M. Robertson

Ordnance
    Lt. Cornelius Gillett **(OR 1:878)**
Headquarters Guard
    32nd Massachusetts Infantry, Company C, Capt. Josiah C. Fuller
First Regular Brigade
Capt. Dunbar R. Ransom
    1st United States, Battery H, Lt. Chandler P. Eakin, Lt. Philip D. Mason
    3rd United States, Batteries F and K, Lieut. John G. Turnbull
    4th United States, Battery C, Lieut. Evan Thomas
    5th United States, Battery C, Lieut. Gulian V. Weir **(OR 1:879)**
First Volunteer Brigade
Lieut. Col. Freeman McGilvery **(OR 1:881)**
    Massachusetts Light, 5th Battery (E), Capt. Charles A. Phillips **(OR 1:884)**
    Massachusetts Light, 9th Battery, Capt. John Bigelow,
        Lt. Richard S. Milton **(OR 1:886)**
    New York Light, 15th Battery, Capt. Patrick Hart **(OR 1:887)**,
        Lt. Andrew R. McMahon **(OR 1:889)
    Pennsylvania Light, Batteries C and F, Capt. James Thompson **(OR 1:889)**
Second Volunteer Brigade
Capt. Elijah D. Taft
    1st Connecticut Heavy, Battery B, Capt. Albert F. Brooker
    1st Connecticut Heavy, Battery M, Capt. Franklin A. Pratt **(OR 1:890)**
    Connecticut Light, 2nd Battery, Capt. John W. Sterling
    New York Light, 5th Battery, Capt. Elijah D. Taft **(OR 1:891)**
Third Volunteer Brigade
Capt. James F. Huntington
    New Hampshire Light, 1st Battery, Capt. Frederick M. Edgell **(OR 1:892)**
    1st Ohio Light, Battery H, Lieut. George W. Norton **(OR 1:893)**
    1st Pennsylvania Light, Batteries F and G, Capt. Bruce Ricketts **(OR 1:894)**
    West Virginia Light, Battery C, Capt. Wallace Hill **(OR 1:895)**
Fourth Volunteer Brigade
Capt. Robert H. Fitzhugh **(OR 1:895)**
    Maine Light, 6th Battery (F), Lt. Edwin B. Dow **(OR 1:897)**

Maryland Light, Battery A, Capt. James H. Rigby **(OR 1:899)**
New Jersey Light, 1st Battery, Lt. Augustin N. Parsons **(OR 1:899)**
1st New York Light, Battery G, Capt. Nelson Ames **(OR 1:900)**
1st New York Light, Battery K, Capt. Robert H. Fitzhugh
Train Guard
4th New Jersey (seven cos.), Maj. Charles Ewing **(OR 1:901)**

Army of Northern Virginia

Gen. Robert E. Lee, commanding. **(OR 2:293)**

First Corps
Lt. Gen. James Longstreet **(OR 2:357)**

McLaws' Division
   Maj. Gen. Lafeyette McLaws
Kershaw's Brigade
Brig. Gen. Kershaw **(OR 2:366)**
   2nd South Carolina, Col. J. D. Kennedy, Lt. Col. F. Gaillard
   3rd South Carolina, Maj. R. C. Maffett **(OR 2:371)**, Col. J. D. Nance **(OR 2:373)**
   7th South Carolina, Col. D. Wyatt Aiken
   8th South Carolina, Col. J. W. Henagan
   15th South Carolina, Col. W. D. De Saussure, Maj. William M. Gist
   3rd South Carolina Battalion, Lt. Col. W. G. Rice
Barksdale's Brigade
Brig. Gen. William Barksdale, Col. B. G. Humphreys
   13th Mississippi, Col. J. W. Carter
   17th Mississippi, Col. W. D. Holder, Lt. Col. John C. Fiser
   18th Mississippi, Col. T. M. Griffin, Lt. Col. W. H. Luse
   21st Mississippi, Col. B. G. Humphreys
Semmes' Brigade
Brig. Gen. P. J. Semmes, Col. Goode Bryan
   10th Georgia, Col. John B. Weems
   50th Georgia, Col. W. R. Manning
   51st Georgia, Col. E. Ball
   53rd Georgia, Col. James P. Simms
Wofford's Brigade
Brig. Gen. W. T. Wofford
   16th Georgia, Col. Goode Bryan
   18th Georgia, Lt. Col. S. Z. Ruff
   24th Georgia, Col. Robert McMillan
   Cobb's (Georgia) Legion, Lt. Col. Luther J. Glenn
   Phillips (Georgia) Legion, Lt. Col. E. S. Barclay
Artillery
Col. H. G. Cabell **(OR 2:374)**
   1st North Carolina Artillery, Battery A, Capt. B. C. Manly **(OR 2:380)**
   Pulaski (Georgia) Artillery, Capt. J. C. Fraser, Lt. W. J. Furlong **(OR 2:381)**
   1st Richmond Howitzers, Capt. E. S. McCarthy **(OR 2:379)**
   Troup (Georgia) Artillery, Capt. H. H. Carlton, Lt. C. W. Motes **(OR 2:384)**

Pickett's Division
    Maj. Gen. George E. Pickett
Garnett's Brigade
Brig. Gen. R. B. Garnett, Maj. C. S. Peyton **(OR 2:385)**
    8th Virginia, Col. Eppa Hunton
    18th Virginia, Lt. Col. H. A. Carrington
    19th Virginia, Col. Henry Gantt, Lt. Col. John T. Ellis
    28th Virginia, Col. R. C. Allen, Lt. Col. William Watts
    56th Virginia, Col. W. D. Stuart, Lt. Col. P. P. Slaughter
Kemper's Brigade
Brig. Gen. J. L. Kemper, Col. Joseph Mayo, Jr.
    1st Virginia, Col. Lewis Williams, Lt. Col. F. G. Skinner
    3rd Virginia, Col. Joseph Mayo, Jr., Lt. Col. A. D. Callcote
    7th Virginia, Col. W. T. Patton, Lt. Col. C. C. Flowerree
    11th Virginia, Maj. Kirkwood Otey
    24th Virginia, Col. William R. Terry
Armistead's Brigade
Brig. Gen. L. A. Armistead, Col. W. R. Aylett
    9th Virginia, Maj. John C. Owens
    14th Virginia, Col. James G. Hodges, Lt. Col. William White
    38th Virginia, Col. E. C. Edmonds, Lt. Col. P. B. Whittle
    53rd Virginia, Col. W. R. Aylett
    57th Virginia, Col. John Bowie Magruder
Artillery
Maj. James Dearing **(OR 2:387)**
    Fauquier (Virginia) Artillery, Capt. R. M. Stribling
    Hampden (Virginia) Artillery, Capt. W. H. Caskie
    Richmond Fayette Artillery, Capt. M. C. Macon
    Virginia Battery, Capt. Joseph G. Blount

Hood's Division
    Maj. Gen. John B. Hood, Brig. Gen. E. M. Law
Law's Brigade
Brig. Gen. E. M. Law, Col. James L. Sheffield
    4th Alabama, Lt. Col. L. H. Scruggs **(OR 2:391)**
    15th Alabama, Col. William C. Oates **(OR 2:444)**, Capt. B. A. Hill
    44th Alabama, Col. William F. Perry **(OR 2:445)**
    47th Alabama, Col. James W. Jackson, Lt. Col. M. J. Bulger,
        Maj. J. M. Campbell **(OR 2:395)**
    48th Alabama, Col. James L. Sheffield **(OR 2:395)**, Capt. T. J. Eubanks
Anderson's Brigade
Brig. Gen. George T. Anderson, Lt. Col. William Luffman
    7th Georgia, Col. W. W. White **(OR 2:396)**
    8th Georgia, Col. John R. Towers
    9th Georgia, Lt. Col. John Mounger, Maj. W. Jones, Capt. Geo. Hillyer **(OR 2:399)**
    11th Georgia, Col. F. H. Little, Lt. Col. William Luffman,
        Maj. Henry D. McDaniel **(OR 2:401)**, Capt. William H. Mitchell
    59th Georgia, Col. Jack Brown, Capt. M. G. Bass, **Maj. B. H. Gee **(OR 2:403)**
Robertson's Brigade
Brig. Gen. J. B. Robertson **(OR 2:404)**
    3rd Arkansas, Col. Van H. Manning **(OR 2:407)**, Lt. Col. R. S. Taylor
    1st Texas, Lt. Col. P. A. Work **(OR 2:408)**

       4th Texas, Col. J. C. G. Key, Maj. J. P. Bane **(OR 2:410)**
       5th Texas, Col. R. M. Powell, Lt. Col. K. Bryan **(OR 2:411)**,
              Maj. J. C. Rogers **(OR 2:413)**
Benning's Brigade
Brig. Gen. Henry L. Benning **(OR 2:414)**
       2nd Georgia, Lt. Col. William T. Harris, Maj. W. S. Shepherd **(OR 2:420)**
       15th Georgia, Col. D. M. DuBose **(OR 2:421)**
       17th Georgia, Col. W. C. Hodges **(OR 2:424)**
       20th Georgia, Col. John A. Jones, Lt. Col. J. D. Waddell **(OR 2:425)**
Artillery
Maj. H. W. Henry **(OR 2:427)**
       Branch (North Carolina) Artillery, Capt. A. C. Latham
       German (South Carolina) Artillery, Capt. William K. Bachman
       Palmetto (South Carolina) Light Artillery, Capt. Hugh R. Garden
       Rowan (North Carolina) Artillery, Capt. James Reilly

ARTILLERY RESERVE
       Col. J. B. Walton
Alexander's Battalion
Col. E. P. Alexander **(OR 2:429)**
       Ashland (Virginia) Artillery, Capt. P. Woolfolk, Jr., Lt. James Woolfolk
       Bedford (Virginia) Artillery, Capt. T. C. Jordan
       Brooks (South Carolina) Artillery, Lt. S. C. Gilbert
       Madison (Louisiana) Light Artillery, Capt. George V. Moody
       Virginia Battery, Capt. W. W. Parker
       Virginia Battery, Capt. O.B. Taylor **(OR 2:431)**
Washington (Louisiana) Artillery
Maj. B. F. Eshleman **(OR 2:433)**
       First Company, Capt. C. W. Squires
       Second Company, Capt. J. B. Richardson
       Third Company, Capt. M. B. Miller
       Fourth Company, Capt. Joe Norcom, Lt. H. A. Battles

Second Corps
Lieut. Gen. Richard S. Ewell **(OR 2:439)**

EARLY'S DIVISION
       Maj. Gen. Jubal A. Early **(OR 2:459)**
Hays' Brigade (The "Louisiana Tigers")
Brig. Gen. Harry T. Hays **(OR 2:476)**
       5th Louisiana, Maj. Alexander Hart, Capt. T. H. Biscoe
       6th Louisiana, Lt. Col. Joseph Hanlon
       7th Louisiana, Col. D. B. Penn
       8th Louisiana, Col. T. D. Lewis, Lt. Col. A. de Blanc, Maj. G. A. Lester
       9th Louisiana, Col. Leroy A. Stafford
Hoke's Brigade
Col. Isaac E. Avery, Col. A. C. Godwin **(OR 2:482)**
       6th North Carolina, Maj. S. McD. Tate **(OR 2:485)**
       21st North Carolina, Col. W. W. Kirkland
       57th North Carolina, Col. A. C. Godwin
Smith's Brigade
Brig. Gen. William Smith
       31st Virginia, Col. John S. Hoffman **(OR 2:488)**

    49th Virginia, Lt. Col. J. Catlett Gibson
    52nd Virginia, Lt. Col. James H. Skinner
Gordon's Brigade
Brig. Gen. J. B. Gordon **(OR 2:491)**
    13th Georgia, Col. James M. Smith
    26th Georgia, Col. E. N. Atkinson
    31st Georgia, Col. Clement A. Evans
    38th Georgia, Capt. William L. McLeod
    60th Georgia, Capt. W. B. Jones
    61st Georgia, Col. John H. Lamar
Artillery
Lt. Col. H. P. Jones **(OR 2:493)**
    Charlottesville (Virginia) Artillery, Capt. James McD. Carrington
    Courtney (Virginia) Artillery, Capt. W. A. Tanner **(OR 2:498)**
    Louisiana Guard Artillery, Capt. C. A. Green **(OR 2:497)**
    Staunton (Virginia) Artillery, Capt. A. W. Garber
JOHNSON'S DIVISION
    Maj. Gen. Edward Johnson **(OR 2:499)**
Steuart's Brigade
Brig. Gen. George H. Steuart **(OR 2:507)**
    1st Maryland Battalion Infantry, Lt. Col. J. R. Herbert,
        Maj. W. W. Goldsborough, Capt. J. P. Crane
    1st North Carolina, Lt. Col. H. A. Brown
    3rd North Carolina, Maj. W. M. Parsley
    10th Virginia, Col. E. T. H. Warren
    23rd Virginia, Lt. Col. S. T. Walton
    37th Virginia, Maj. H. C. Wood
Nicholls' Brigade
Col. J. M. Williams **(OR 2:512)**
    1st Louisiana, Capt. E. D. Willett **(OR 2:514)**
    2nd Louisiana, Lt. Col. R. E. Burke
    10th Louisiana, Maj. T. N. Powell **(OR 2:514)**
    14th Louisiana, Lt. Col. David Zable **(OR 2:514)**
    15th Louisiana, Maj. Andrew Brady **(OR 2:515)**
Stonewall Brigade
Brig. Gen. James A. Walker **(OR 2:515)**
    2nd Virginia, Col. J. Q. A. Nadenbousch **(OR 2:519)**
    4th Virginia, Maj. William Terry **(OR 2:522)**
    5th Virginia, Col. J. H. S. Funk **(OR 2:526)**
    27th Virginia, Lieut. Col. D. M. Shriver **(OR 2:527)**
    33rd Virginia, Capt. J. B. Golladay **(OR 2:528)**
Jones' Brigade
Brig. Gen. John M. Jones **(OR 2:531)**, Lt. Col. R. H. Dungan **(OR 2:533)**,
    Col. Bradley T. Johnson **(OR 2:534)
    21st Virginia, Capt. W. P. Moseley **(OR 2:535)**
    25th Virginia, Col. J. C. Higginbotham **(OR 2:536)**, Lt. Col. J. A. Robinson
    42nd Virginia, Lt. Col. R. W. Withers, Capt. S. H. Saunders,
        Capt. Jesse M. Richardson **(OR 2:536)
    44th Virginia, Maj. N. Cobb, Capt. T. R. Buckner **(OR 2:538)**
    48th Virginia, Lt. Col. R. H. Dungan, Maj. Oscar White
    50th Virginia, Lt. Col. L. H. N. Salyer **(OR 2:538)**

Artillery
Maj. J. Latimer **(OR 2:540)**, Capt. C. Raine, **Col. Snowden Andrews **(OR 2:543)**
    1st Maryland Battery, Capt. William F. Dement
    Alleghany (Virginia) Artillery, Capt. J. C. Carpenter
    Chesapeake (Maryland) Artillery, Capt. William D. Brown
    Lee (Virginia) Battery, Capt. C. I. Raine, Lt. William W. Hardwicke

RODES' DIVISION
    Maj. Gen. R. E. Rodes **(OR 2:545)**
Battalion of Sharpshooters
Maj. Eugene Blackford **(OR 2:597)**
Daniel's Brigade
Brig. Gen. Junius Daniel **(OR 2:564)**
    32nd North Carolina, Col. E. C. Brabble **(OR 2:571)**
    43rd North Carolina, Col. T. S. Kenan, Lt. Col. W. G. Lewis **(OR 2:572)**
    45th North Carolina, Lt. Col. S. H. Boyd, Maj. John R. Winston,
        Capt. A. H. Gallaway, Capt. J. A. Hopkins **(OR 2:574)**
    53rd North Carolina, Col. W. A. Owens **(OR 2:576)**
    2nd North Carolina Battalion, Lt. Col. H. L. Andrews,
        Capt. Van Brown **(OR 2:577)**
Iverson's Brigade
Brig. Gen. Alfred Iverson **(OR 2:578)**
    5th North Carolina, Capt. Speight B. West, Capt. Benjamin Robinson
    12th North Carolina, Lt. Col. W. S. Davis
    20th North Carolina, Lt. Col. Nelson Slough, Capt. Lewis T. Hicks
    23rd North Carolina, Col. D. H. Christie, Capt. William H. Johnston
Doles' Brigade
Brig. Gen. George Doles **(OR 2:581)**
    4th Georgia, Lt. Col. D. R. E. Winn, Maj. W. H. Willis **(OR 2:584)**
    12th Georgia, Col. Edward Willis
    21st Georgia, Col. John T. Mercer **(OR 2:584)**
    44th Georgia, Col. S. P. Lumpkin, Maj. W. H. Peebles **(OR 2:585)**
Ramseur's Brigade
Brig. Gen. S. D. Ramseur **(OR 2:587)**
    2nd North Carolina, Maj. D. W. Hurtt, Capt. James T. Scales,
        Capt. Orren Williams **(OR 2:589)
    4th North Carolina, Col. Bryan Grimes **(OR 2:589)**
    14th North Carolina, Col. Tyler Bennett, Maj. Joseph Lambeth **(OR 2:590)**
    30th North Carolina, Col. Francis M. Parker, Maj. W. W. Sillers **(OR 2:591)**
O'Neal's Brigade
Col. E. A. O'Neal **(OR 2:591)**
    3rd Alabama, Col. C. A. Battle **(OR 2:594)**
    5th Alabama, Col. J. M. Hall **(OR 2:595)**
    6th Alabama, Col. J. N. Lightfoot, Capt. M. L. Bowie **(OR 2:599)**
    12th Alabama, Col. S. B. Pickens **(OR 2:600)**
    26th Alabama, Lt. Col. John C. Goodgame **(OR 2:601)**
Artillery
Lieut. Col. Thomas H. Carter **(OR 2:602)**
    Jeff. Davis (Alabama) Artillery, Capt. W. J. Reese
    King William (Virginia) Artillery, Capt. W. P. Carter
    Morris (Virginia) Artillery, Capt. R. C. M. Page
    Orange (Virginia) Artillery, Capt. C. W. Fry

ARTILLERY RESERVE
    Col. J. Thompson Brown **(OR 2:455)**
Ordnance
Lt. John M. Gregory, Jr. **(OR 2:458)**
    First Virginia Artillery, Capt. Willis J. Dance **(OR 2:604)**
    2nd Richmond (Virginia) Howitzers, Capt. David Watson
    3rd Richmond (Virginia) Howitzers, Capt. B. H. Smith, Jr.
    Powhatan (Virginia) Artillery, Lt. John M. Cunningham
    Rockbridge (Virginia) Artillery, Capt. A. Graham
    Salem (Virginia) Artillery, Lt. C. B. Griffin
Nelson's Battalion
Lt. Col. William Nelson **(OR 2:605)**
    Amherst (Virginia) Artillery, Capt. T. J. Kirkpatrick
    Fluvanna (Virginia) Artillery, Capt. J. L. Massie
    Georgia Battery, Capt. John Milledge, Jr.

Third Corps
Lt. Gen. Ambrose P. Hill **(OR 2:606)**

ANDERSON'S DIVISION
    Maj. Gen. R. H. Anderson **(OR 2:612)**
Wilcox's Brigade
Brig. Gen. Cadmus M. Wilcox **(OR 2:616)**
    8th Alabama, Lt. Col. Hilary A. Herbert
    9th Alabama, Capt. J. H. King
    10th Alabama, Col. William H. Forney, Lt. Col. James E. Shelley
    11th Alabama, Col. J. C. C. Sanders, Lt. Col. George E. Tayloe
    14th Alabama, Col. L. Pinkard, Lt. Col. James A. Broome
Mahone's Brigade
Brig. Gen. William Mahone **(OR 2:621)**
    6th Virginia, Col. George T. Rogers
    12th Virginia, Col. D. A. Weisiger
    16th Virginia, Col. Joseph H. Ham
    41st Virginia, Col. William A. Parham
    61st Virginia, Col. V. D. Groner
Wright's Brigade
Brig. Gen. A. R. Wright **(OR 2:622)**, Col. William Gibson
    3rd Georgia, Col. E. J. Walker **(OR 2:627)**
    22nd Georgia, Col. Joseph Wasden, Capt. B. C. McCurry **(OR 2:628)**
    48th Georgia, Col. William Gibson, Capt. M. R. Hall **(OR 2:629)**,
        Col. William Gibson
    2nd Georgia Battalion, Maj. George Ross, Capt. Charles Moffett **(OR 2:630)**
Perry's Brigade
Col. David Lang **(OR 2:631)**
    2nd Florida, Maj. W. R. Moore
    5th Florida, Capt. R. N. Gardner
    8th Florida, Col. David Lang
Posey's Brigade
Brig. Gen. Carnot Posey **(OR 2:633)**
    12th Mississippi, Col. W. H. Taylor
    16th Mississippi, Col. Samuel E. Baker
    19th Mississippi, Col. N. H. Harris **(OR 2:634)**
    48th Mississippi, Col. Joseph M. Jayne

Artillery (Sumter Battalion)
Maj. John Lane **(OR 2:635)**
    Company A, Capt. Hugh M. Ross
    Company B, Capt. George M. Patterson
    Company C, Capt. John T. Wingfield

HETH'S DIVISION
    Maj. Gen. Henry Heth **(OR 2:637)**, Brig. Gen. J. J. Pettigrew
First Brigade
Brig. Gen. J. J. Pettigrew, Col. J. K. Marshall, **Maj. J. Jones **(OR 2:642)**
    11th North Carolina, Col. Collett Leventhorpe
    26th North Carolina, Col. Henry K. Burgwyn, Jr., Capt. H. C. Albright,
        *Capt. J. J. Young **(OR 2:645)**
    47th North Carolina, Col. G. H. Faribault
    52nd North Carolina, Col. J. K. Marshall, Lt. Col. Marcus A. Parks
Second Brigade
Col. J. M. Brockenbrough
    40th Virginia, Capt. T. E. Betts, Capt. R. B. Davis
    47th Virginia, Col. Robert M. Mayo
    55th Virginia, Col. W. S. Christian
    22nd Virginia Battalion, Maj. John S. Bowles
Third Brigade
Brig. Gen. James J. Archer, Col. B. D. Fry, Lt. Col. S. G. Shepard **(OR 2:646)**
    13th Alabama, Col. B. D. Fry
    5th Alabama Battalion, Maj. A. S. Van de Graaf
    1st Tennessee (Provisional Army), Maj. Felix G. Buchanan.
    7th Tennessee, Lt. Col. S. G. Shepard
    14th Tennessee, Capt. B. L. Phillips
Fourth Brigade
Brig. Gen. Joseph R. Davis **(OR 2:648)**
    2nd Mississippi, Col. J. M. Stone
    11th Mississippi, Col. F. M. Green
    42nd Mississippi, Col. H. R. Miller
    55th North Carolina, Col. J. K. Connally
Artillery
Lt. Col. John J. Garnett **(OR 2:652)**, **Maj. Charles Richardson **(OR 2:654)**
    Donaldson (Louisiana) Artillery, Capt. V. Maurin
    Huger (Virginia) Artillery, Capt. Joseph D. Moore
    Lewis (Virginia) Artillery, Capt. John W. Lewis
    Norfolk Light Artillery Blues, Capt. C. R. Grandy

PENDER'S DIVISION
    Maj. Gen. William D. Pender, Brig. Gen. James H. Lane,
        Maj. Gen. I. R. Trimble, *Maj. Joseph A. Engelhard **(OR 2:656)**
First Brigade
Col. Abner Perrin **(OR 2:660)**
    1st South Carolina (Provisional Army), Maj. C. W. McCreary
    1st South Carolina Rifles, Capt. William M. Hadden
    12th South Carolina, Col. John L. Miller
    13th South Carolina, Lt. Col. B. T. Brockman
    14th South Carolina, Lt. Col. Joseph N. Brown
Second Brigade
Brig. Gen. James H. Lane **(OR 2:664)**, Col. C. M. Avery

7th North Carolina, Capt. J. McLeod Turner, Capt. James G. Harris
18th North Carolina, Col. John D. Barry
28th North Carolina, Col. S. D. Lowe, Lt. Col. W. H. A. Speer
33rd North Carolina, Col. C. M. Avery
37th North Carolina, Col. W. M. Barbour

Third Brigade
Brig. Gen. Edward L. Thomas **(OR 2:668)**
    14th Georgia, Col. Robert W. Folsom
    35th Georgia, Col. Bolling H. Holt
    45th Georgia, Col. T. J. Simmons
    49th Georgia, Col. S. T. Player

Fourth Brigade
Brig. Gen. A. M. Scales **(OR 2:669)**, Lt. Col. G. T. Gordon,
    Col. W. Lee J. Lowrance **(OR 2:671)**
    13th North Carolina, Col. J. H. Hyman, Lt. Col. H. A. Rogers
    16th North Carolina, Capt. L. W. Stowe
    22nd North Carolina, Col. James Conner
    34th North Carolina, Col. William Lee J. Lowrance, Lt. Col. G. T. Gordon
    38th North Carolina, Col. W. J. Hoke, Lt. Col. John Ashford.

Artillery
Maj. William T. Poague **(OR 2:673)**
    Albemarle (Virginia) Artillery, Capt. James W. Wyatt
    Charlotte (North Carolina) Artillery, Capt. Joseph Graham
    Madison (Mississippi) Light Artillery, Capt. George Ward
    Virginia Battery, Capt. J. V. Brooke

ARTILLERY RESERVE
    Col. R. Lindsay Walker **(OR 2:609)**

McIntosh's Battalion
Maj. D. G. McIntosh **(OR 2:674)**
    Danville (Virginia) Artillery, Capt. R. S. Rice
    Hardaway (Alabama) Artillery, Capt. W. B. Hurt
    2nd Rockbridge (Virginia) Artillery, Lt. Samuel Wallace
    Virginia Battery, Capt. M. Johnson

Pegram's Battalion
Maj. W. J. Pegram, Capt. E. B. Brunson **(OR 2:677)**
    Crenshaw (Virginia) Battery, Capt. W. G. Crenshaw
    Fredericksburg (Virginia) Artillery, Capt. E. A. Marye
    Letcher (Virginia) Artillery, Capt. T. Brander
    Pee Dee (South Carolina) Artillery, Lt. William E. Zimmerman
    Purcell (Virginia) Artillery, Capt. Joseph McGraw

Cavalry

STUART'S DIVISION
    Maj. Gen. J. E. B. Stuart **(OR 2:679)**

Hampton's Brigade
Brig. Gen. Wade Hampton **(OR 2:721)**, Col. L. S. Baker
    1st North Carolina, Col. L. S. Baker
    1st South Carolina, Col. J. L. Black
    2nd South Carolina, Col. M. C. Butler
    Cobb's (Georgia) Legion, Col. P. B. M. Young
    Jeff. Davis Legion, Col. J. F. Waring

Phillips (Georgia) Legion, Lt. Col. J. C. Phillips
Robertson's Brigade
Brig. Gen. Beverly H. Robertson
    4th North Carolina, Col. D. D. Ferebee
    5th North Carolina, Col. P. G. Evans
Fitz. Lee's Brigade
Brig. Gen. Fitz. Lee.
    1st Maryland Battalion, Maj. Harry Gilmor, Maj. Ridgely Brown
    1st Virginia, Col. James H. Drake
    2nd Virginia, Col. T. T. Munford
    3rd Virginia, Col. Thomas H. Owen
    4th Virginia, Col. Williams C. Wickham
    5th Virginia, Col. T. L. Rosser
Jenkins' Brigade
Brig. Gen. A. G. Jenkins, Col. M. J. Ferguson
    14th Virginia, Maj. B. F. Eakle
    16th Virginia, Col. M. J. Ferguson
    17th Virginia, Col. W. H. French
    34th Virginia Battalion, Lt. Col. V. A. Witcher
    36th Virginia Battalion, Capt. C. T. Smith
    Jackson's (Virginia) Battery, Capt. Thomas E. Jackson
Jones' Brigade
Brig. Gen. William E. Jones **(OR 2:748)**
    6th Virginia, Maj. C. E. Flournoy **(OR 2:754)**
    7th Virginia, Lt. Col. Thomas Marshall **(OR 2:757)**
    11th Virginia, Col. L. L. Lomax **(OR 2:762)**
W. H. F. Lee's Brigade
Col. J. R. Chambliss, Jr.
    2nd North Carolina, Lt. Joseph Baker
    9th Virginia, Col. R. L. T. Beale
    10th Virginia, Col. J. Lucius Davis
    13th Virginia, Capt. B. F. Winfield
Stuart Horse Artillery
Maj. R. F. Beckham
    Breathed's (Virginia) Battery, Capt. James Breathed
    Chew's (Virginia) Battery, Capt. R. P. Chew
    Griffin's (Maryland) Battery, Capt. W. H. Griffin
    Hart's (South Carolina) Battery, Capt. J. F. Hart
    McGregor's (Virginia) Battery, Capt. W. M. McGregor
    Moorman's (Virginia) Battery, Capt. M. N. Moorman

IMBODEN'S COMMAND
Brig. Gen. J. D. Imboden
    18th Virginia Cavalry, Col. George W. Imboden
    62nd Virginia Infantry, Col. George H. Smith
    Virginia Partisan Rangers, Capt. John H. McNeill
    Virginia Battery, Capt. J. H. McClanahan

ARTILLERY
    Brig. Gen. W. N. Pendleton **(OR 2:346)**

ORDNANCE
    Lt. Col. Briscoe G. Baldwin **(OR 2:357)**